S0-BSY-515

Some Gave All

Some Gave All

A History of Baltimore Police Officers Killed in the Line of Duty 1808–2007

STEVEN P. OLSON

and ROBERT P. BROWN

Foreword by
CHRISTOPHER DREISBACH

Fraternal Order of Police
Memorial Fund Committee

BALTIMORE, MARYLAND
2007

Library of Congress Cataloging-in-Publication Data

Olson, Steven P., 1972-
Some gave all : a history of Baltimore police officers killed in the line of duty 1808-2007 / Steven P. Olson and Robert P. Brown; foreword by Christopher Dreisbach.
p. cm.
Includes bibliographical references and index.
ISBN 978-0-9635159-5-7 (alk. paper)
1. Police—Mortality—Maryland—Baltimore. 2. Police—Violence against—Maryland—Baltimore 3. Baltimore (Md.) Police Dept.—History. I. Olson, Steven P., 1972- II. Title.
HV8148.B22B76 2007
364.15209752'6—dc22 2007011900

Manufactured in the United States of America.
The paper used in this publication meets the minimum requirements of the American National Standard for Information Sciences Permanence of Paper for Printed Library Materials
ANSI Z39.48-1984.

Produced for the Baltimore Fraternal Order of Police
Memorial Fund Committee by the
Chesapeake Book Company
Baltimore, Maryland, 410.467.2269
For orders in the book trade contact Alan C. Hood & Co., Inc.,
Chambersburg, Pennsylvania
hoodbooks@pa.net 717.267.0867

Funding provided by
The Fraternal Order of Police Memorial Board,
Baltimore, Maryland

All proceeds from the sale of this book will be dedicated to the maintainenance and care of the Police Memorial at the intersection of Fayette and President Streets, Baltimore.

Fraternal Order of Police Memorial Board

For Laura and Brooke

Contents

Foreword

Greater love has no one than this, that he lay down his life for his friends.

—John 15:13 NIV

"Some call him pig," declared a billboard in St. Paul, Minnesota, in the late 1960s. Accompanying this observation was a picture of a police officer administering CPR to a toddler. The message was clear: in spite of a few cops out of control, the counter-culture was wrong to see the police as the enemy. Part of the problem was that loud and persistent detractors were ubiquitous in all forms of media, while police officers who went about their business insuring our safety and security were not doing anything newsworthy enough to be recognized. Of course, the media were all over the bad cop, and so the ordinary citizen who never needed an officer's assistance was left with the mistaken image of an unprofessional force of hooligans. That an occasional news report told of a police officer killed in the line of duty did little to elevate the general attitude toward the profession.

Then came September 11, 2001, since which infamous day the popular attitude toward law enforcement has improved considerably. As our sense of vulnerability has increased, so has our understanding and appreciation that police are our first line of defense against harm. Nevertheless, the media continue to present exceptional images of police as if they were the rule. While police who are the subject of news stories are either extraordinary heroes or startling miscreants, most of the excellent work performed by the agents of law enforcement continues to be done without fanfare or profound public consequences and thus without being newsworthy. On the whole, police are *ordinary* heroes. For those of us in direct need of police assistance, they are there within minutes of our request. For those of us who have made it through another day without becoming a victim of crime, we have in large part the vigilance of the police to thank. We may never need to call on them for help, and we may never know them by name, but they have dedicated their lives to keeping us safe and secure, even to the extent of laying down their lives. Pigs no; friends yes.

In this book, Robert Brown and Steven Olson offer a series of vignettes reminding us of the ultimate expression of police dedication. Each story tells of an officer killed in the line of duty. In some cases the death was accidental, in others intentional and often malicious. In all cases the outcome is the same: a police officer dies and we are the poorer for it. But that loss is also an occasion for celebration. As the Greek and Roman stoics reminded us, life is like a banquet to which we have been invited without having earned that invitation. We may not like all of the food the banquet offers, there may not be enough of the foods we like, we may not like all of the company, and there is no guarantee of how long we can stay. Yet there will be foods we like and guests we come to cherish. When the time comes to leave, our proper response is not to demand more time but to thank the host for having invited us in the first place. Similarly, if another guest whom we like has to leave before us, we should not mourn that loss so much as thank the host for having invited him or her. Thus, even as we acknowledge the tragedy and the poignancy of the stories in this excellent book, we should take them as reminders to ourselves of the wonderful gifts of life and the people who live to make our lives better.

For each officer depicted in this book, it may be appropriate to observe a moment of silence. But then it is perfectly all right to celebrate the fact that posterity has given us these police professionals, these ordinary heroes, these friends.

Christopher Dreisbach, Ph.D.
Division of Public Safety Leadership
The Johns Hopkins University

Preface

Bobby and I settled into a table with a window view looking out onto Pratt Street. We hadn't known each other before early 2003, but we had a common purpose and drive. In the country's oldest Irish Pub, Patrick's of Pratt Street, across from the B&O Railroad Museum, we ordered a couple of Guinness pints and started to talk. New customers have the pleasure and obligation of introducing themselves to the owners, Patrick and Anne, before enjoying good beer and great food. The original ornate woodwork of the bar and decorative ceiling lent themselves to the discussion of Baltimore history.

After years of policing, Bobby explained that he had begun to look at the memorial plaques that hung on station house walls in a new way. He would ponder the possible circumstances that surrounded the deaths of his fellow officers. These large, badge-shaped plaques gave little more than names, ranks, assignments, dates of service and death. A very skilled researcher, he began to search the numerous archives and libraries for details. Over several years of slow and arduous work, he amassed a large file of information. He kept copies of articles, death certificates, and official records in a large gray plastic box which did little more than sit and take up room.

His twelve years of policing more than doubled my own experience, and I related to him how I had begun to involve myself in the very same pursuit of knowledge only months before. At the time, I was assigned to the Education and Training Section teaching self-defense. A recent, serious injury put me behind a desk with little more to do than busy work. I also had seen these plaques hanging in the districts and thought some of the very same things. At the request of Lt. Fred Roussey and Sgt. Ron Dorsey, I began to compile a list of officers killed in the line of duty to put on display, reminding us of those who had sacrificed their lives in defense of our city.

A task that I thought would take one phone call to the Personnel Section and a day to complete turned into a major project. I compared the lists from the Fraternal Order of Police, the National Law Enforcement Memorial and the official department records and discovered they didn't match. Like Bobby, I decided to research and create a definitive memorial to honor those who came before us.

A friend heard of my project—it is a blessing to be part of the large police family—and introduced me to Bobby. With his help, we were able to quickly compile a complete list. "A simple list isn't good enough," Bobby said, "If you want people to remember, we have to tell them what happened." I agreed. As we sat drinking another pint, this book began to shape itself in our minds. Bobby would research and I would write. Years before we finished, we became very good friends. We were excited and humbled to shoulder the daunting task of putting together the following stories, but we found support from everyone we knew, especially our families.

Bobby's family ties its history to Baltimore after his grandmother moved to this city from North Carolina. His love of genealogy and research complemented my own love of history. Although I am not a Baltimorean by birth, my wife's family has for many generations been a large component of the city's social and commercial fabric.

Our goal with this book is to keep a promise the police family makes to all of its brothers and sisters who die in the line of duty—to ensure that posterity never forgets the sacrifices they made.

Acknowledgments

It is difficult to acknowledge everyone who has had an impact on our efforts to complete such an emotionally taxing book. Although we spent many hours in libraries and offices sifting through overwhelming amounts of material, there are several people who heard of our project and offered their time, expertise, experience and support.

First and foremost are our wives and families. Laura and Brooke offered fresh perspective, new ideas, and understanding. For Laura it meant losing Bobby to libraries and archives; for Brooke it meant endless requests to read passages and listen to ideas. Bobby's sons, Christopher Walrath, Jeremy, Joshua, and Andrew Brown, showed their support for their father by taking genuine interest in his research. Patricia Scarlett Hopkins, Steven's mother-in-law, spent much of her personal time, reading and editing the entire project and still found time to provide holiday meals to Northern District officers who worked on Thanksgiving and Christmas. Her efforts directly influenced the final form of our work. Bert and Anthea Smith contributed their professional and technical expertise from the very beginning.

In addition, Maj. Ed Schmidt, Donald "Chic" Matthews, and Charlene F. DePasquale of the Baltimore Police Department, Personnel Section, made it possible for us to comb through the department's official records. Retired Sergeant Robert Fischer encouraged Bobby in the initial stages of his research and Officer Bob Basiliere donated much of his own material to help. Maj. Regis L. Phelan, Lt. Fred Roussey, Gene Cassidy, and Bob Anderson stepped outside of their official roles in the department to lend support and became friends as a result.

Chris Cosgriff, the founder of the "Officer Down Memorial Page," on the Internet, provided many of the fallen officers' pictures and helped to uncover previously unrecognized heroes. Steve's best friend, Justin Reynolds, spent hours with him in the Maryland Room of the Enoch Pratt Free Library, searching through seemingly endless reels of microfilm. Funding for the book was provided by the Fraternal Order of Police Lodge #3 and the Memorial Fund Committee.

Bobby and Steve are especially grateful for the close friends and family members of those officers who were killed in the line of duty and took the time to relate the personal stories and touching memories that give this book its true voice. Their stories were often followed by tears, smiles, and hugs.

Steven P. Olson
Robert P. Brown
Baltimore, January 2007

— Fallen Officers —

Night Watchman George Workner

March 15, 1808
Middle District

On the night of March 14, 1808, George Workner became the first officer to be killed in the line of duty while protecting the citizens of Baltimore. Known as Baltimore Town, the bustling port and growing hub of trade on the Atlantic Coast of the new republic was also a magnet for violent criminals. In an attempt to maintain order, the city adopted laws with tough penalties, and with the establishment of an organized body of night watchmen in the harbor area laid the foundation for its police department.

But on that March night, George Workner lay on his back on the cold stone floor of Baltimore's jail and held his hands tightly over the burning knife wound in his side as all around him escaping prisoners battled with their guards. Daniel Doherty and fellow conspirators James Swincher, William Robinson, Dick Bowser, Will Bell, Paraway Johnson, Caleb Doherty, William Morris, and a man simply named Moses had fashioned keys out of pewter to pick the locks of their cells and had somehow secured the knife to aid their escape. They had orchestrated their efforts, then rushed the unsuspecting night watchman and the guards as they went about their daily responsibilities. It was Daniel Doherty who had wounded Workner with the small, three-inch blade, leaving him to die the next day.

After the battle, which left several men wounded and Workner dying, the prisoners made their way to temporary freedom. In the absence of an effective, well-trained police force, the newspapers pleaded for citizens to apprehend the escaped convicts. The danger was great, but townspeople arrested the nine escapees one by one. All had been convicted of serious crimes and faced lengthy prison sentences. All had been sentenced to "the roads," the popular term for a chain gang. Once recaptured, four of the nine—Morris, Robinson, Daniel Doherty, and Caleb Doherty—were sentenced to hang for their part in Workner's murder. Two days before their execution, the four made another unsuccessful attempt to escape. In a written appeal for clemency, Morris explained, "We would all rather die in combat than suspended by a cord." At noon on April 22, 1808, the four "were launched into an awful eternity."

In 1859 the original Baltimore Jail was torn to the ground to make way for a more secure stone structure. Today, dwarfed by the enormous walls of a modern jail and the high double bridges of the Jones Falls Expressway, the old jail still commands respect from the onlooker for its eye-catching architecture. Its stone face, darkened over time, with the gentle light gray curves of the main door's arch, is highlighted by twin columns that remind people of a medieval castle. Now in the heart of the city, it was, during Workner's time, when Baltimore covered a mere sixty-four acres, on the city's outskirts. A single, bloody act within a structure no longer standing marked the first violent episode in the proud history of the Baltimore City Police Department.

Night Watchman John O'Mayer

November 14, 1856
Eastern District

The tension had mounted for some time prior to Election Day, November 3, 1856. Factions employed gangs of young men who battled in the streets in the service of candidates for political office. The American Party threatened the status quo by publicly denouncing slavery. As Tracy Matthew Melton wrote in, *Hanging Henry Gambrill,* the fear was that "if Maryland goes for [the Presidential Candidate Millard] Fillmore, she *loses* her Southern character, and with it Baltimore loses her Southern *capital* and Southern *customers.*" In this tense atmosphere, the Democrats and the American Party, also called the Know-Nothings, paid members of such gangs as the Plug Uglies, Rip Raps, Rough Skins, Tigers and Black Snakes to intimidate potential voters. In a few years, Maryland would be a battleground for large armies, but in October and November 1856, Baltimore was already the scene of open warfare.

At the appointed time on November 3, the polling places opened their doors and men went about the business of running an election. It would not be long before violence seized the whole of the city. With wanton disregard for the lives of their fellow man, opposing gangs began to trade gunfire in the streets. Newspapers listed the dead and wounded in lengthy columns. Most disturbing were the names of innocent men, women, and children who had been caught in the crossfire. When men choose to battle, there is sympathy for their deaths and injuries, but those who are innocent and are killed and maimed bring a new feeling of loss.

The scene of the worst violence was the Bel Air Market. The Sixth Ward Ashland American Club along with the Seventh Ward Jefferson American Club raised their fists, pistols, muskets, and even small cannons against the Democrats of the Empire Club and Eighth Ward Jackson Club. Using the techniques of a modern army in combat, opposing forces in the market "fired perfect volleys of musketry and the occasional discharge of a swivel." An immediate alarm was sent to the nearest police station house and the men of the Eastern District responded. Anticipating the violence of the day, Mayor Samuel Hinks ordered the night watch to be held over as increased security and a potential reserve force. Among those men was Night Watchman John O'Mayer.

When the call came in to stop the violence at the Bel Air Market, the city's police found themselves fighting both sides of the conflict in a difficult attempt to stem the combat. Ten officers were shot in the action, most of whom suffered minor injuries. O'Mayer's wound was accidental as he shot himself in his own hand. For several days after, the men of the Eastern District recovered from their "ugly but not dangerous" wounds, but O'Mayer's conditioned worsened when infection set in and spread quickly. When it was apparent that the infection threatened the watchman's life, Dr. Yates, the treating physician, amputated his hand.

The operation was too late and the infection grew into a severe case of lockjaw. On November 13, 1856, John O'Mayer died at his home with his wife and child by his side. The funeral was held on November 15, and he was given the honors bestowed upon a soldier when "the military fired three volleys over the grave and the cortege retired." The leaders of the city mourned the death of the watchman by flying the flags at half-staff.

SERGEANT WILLIAM JOURDAN

Middle District, October 14, 1857

In the mid-1800s, Baltimore struggled to find a political identity. Elections were occasions for violence. The nativist American or Know Nothing Party opposed to immigrants and the Catholic Church engaged the Democratic Party in gun battles and street fighting for control of the polling places, only one of which was located in each ward. In 1857 alone, the police arrested and charged 8,949 people for shooting at police officers. Even though the department was charged with maintaining order, the very people the police tried to keep from harming one another turned their guns on them. On October 14, 1857, this violence took the life of Sergeant William Jourdan.

Early in the morning, voters had gathered on Gay Street near Front Street to cast their ballots at the Fifth Ward polls. In an attempt to maintain order, several Democratic candidates withdrew their names from consideration for seats on the city council. This served to quiet some of the trouble that had been brewing, but it did not prevent the shooting of Sergeant Jourdan. About half past one in the afternoon, with the streets filled with voters and political activists, a man on the roof of an omnibus fired a pistol into the crowd. After the shooting stopped, many of the onlookers chased after him. The shooter ran through a store owned by Jehu Gorsuch at the corner of Front and Gay Streets, then onto the roof of that store, and finally escaped by descending through an adjacent house. Fighting erupted in the street.

The situation demanded immediate action by the police officers on scene to keep the fight from turning into a riot. Fortunately for the police, one group involved in the altercation retreated down High Street toward French Street. Wanting the retreat to continue, the police did what they could to push them further. As police encouraged the crowd to keep moving, more shots rang out from a window of Democratic headquarters, Jackson Hall. One ball found Sergeant Jourdan, who died a few minutes later. Lieutenant Carmichael took charge, and transported Jourdan's body to his house.

Nearly 250 officers attended Sergeant Jourdan's funeral from the Middle, Southern and Western Districts. At three o'clock on October 15, 1857, a procession led by fellow officers carried his body from his home on Ann Street near Eastern Avenue to the Baltimore Cemetery. When his death was reported in the *Baltimore Sun*, he was remembered as "a faithful officer one who ever performed his duty with zeal for the good order of society and the peace of the city."

PATROLMAN BENJAMIN BENTON

Western District, September 22, 1858

PATROLMAN ROBERT M. RIGDON

Western District, November 5, 1858

On the warm night of September 22, 1858, Officer Wesley Burke walked the streets and alleyways, keeping a watchful eye on the citizens and property of the city's west end. As he walked, he swung his nightstick in a manner that kept his mind and hands occupied.

Late in the evening, he came upon what appeared to be a dance or some sort of amusement in a house on Biddle Street, near Pennsylvania Avenue. As he approached, he noticed a large group of young men on the walk outside the house, trying to get inside while the hostess struggled to keep them out. Burke realized he needed help and double-rapped his nightstick against the brick wall of a building. Fellow officers Benjamin Benton, Robert Rigdon, and J. L. Brown heard the distinctive call of an officer's espantoon and responded immediately.

The four officers decided to arrest two of the rowdy bunch and put their hands on David Houck and John Isenhart. Henry Gambrill, one of the leaders of the young men causing the disturbance, attempted to free Houck, then stepped back. A pistol suddenly appeared, leveled at Officer Benton's head. From three feet away, the assailant pulled the trigger. Officer Benton fell to the ground, never knowing who had killed him. Houck and the assailants fled the scene. Benton's partners Rigdon, Brown, and Burke did their best to help their friend, but could not save him. Gambrill, Houck, and Isenhart were tracked down and arrested shortly after by Captain Linaweaver.

The next day, a grand jury indicted Gambrill for Benton's murder. Justice Logan immediately incarcerated Gambrill. Barely two months later, with the events fresh in his mind, Rigdon testified before a jury, describing the turmoil, confusion, and bloodshed surrounding the death of his friend. He named Gambrill as the shooter. After his testimony he reported to roll call and returned home. Rigdon's wife was tending the store in the front of their house at 468 West Baltimore Street when Peter Corrie entered, pretending both drunkenness and sympathy.

Rigdon eyed Corrie with suspicion but did not recognize the extent of the danger he presented and remained in the back room. His wife asked his help in removing Corrie, but Rigdon, wary and wanting to maintain what he thought was a position of advantage, called out that he would not come forward. Rigdon was unaware that Corrie's partner, Marion "Mal" Cropp, was hiding in the alley just outside his window. As Rigdon waited, preparing for whatever threat might come through the front door, Cropp pointed his pistol through the back window and fired. The single blast sent five balls into Rigdon's back. Both Cropp and Corrie ran from the scene. Officer John Cook, who was in the area, gave chase in a running gun battle, and caught up with Corrie. When Corrie was apprehended he immediately asserted his innocence and said, "Marion Cropp did it."

Because of Officer Rigdon's testimony, Henry Gambrill was found guilty* of the murder of Benjamin Benton. On January 26, 1859, a jury also convicted Corrie and Cropp of the revenge murder of Officer Robert Rigdon. The three men were sentenced to "be hung by the neck until they be dead." On April 8, 1859, the trio, together with a fourth man, John Stephens, also known as "Cephus," were executed in a quadruple hanging. Thousands crowded the hillsides surrounding the jail to view the spectacle. The city council voted to give the wives of the two officers a full year's salary, $520, in order to help meet expenses.

*In 1866, Richard Harris, with Gambrill a member of the Plug Uglies club, confessed on his deathbed to shooting Benton. See Tracy Matthew Melton, *Hanging Henry Gambrill: The Violent Career of Baltimore's Plug Uglies, 1854–1860* (Baltimore: Maryland Historical Society, 2005), 407–9.

Patrolman James Murphy

Western District, July 5, 1870
3 months of service

July 4, 1870, was a typically hot Baltimore summer afternoon. Officer Murphy was on patrol in the Lexington Market, charged with keeping the peace. About three o'clock he confronted the Duering brothers for acting in a "disorderly and riotous manner." The brothers, John, James, and David, were warned that if they continued in their conduct they were going to be arrested. James Duering ignored Murphy's warning and continued to disturb the peace.

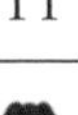

When Murphy subsequently arrested James and tried to take him to the station house, John and David Duering set upon him with their fists and wrestled James from his custody. Officer Murphy chased them on foot along Paca Street while summoning help from his fellow officers. Once he caught up with them, Officer Murphy regained his control over James but again could not defend himself from the two other Duering brothers who attacked him, this time with clubs.

The attack broke off, and the brothers fled when they saw two officers running to aid Officer Murphy. Officer Murphy held onto James while Officers Mantle and Engle chased his brothers. Officer Mantle caught David, who attempted to hide in an outhouse, and Officer Engle found John hiding in his mother's house on Orchard Street.

Eventually, all three brothers were brought to the Western Station House, formally charged with the assault on Officer Murphy, and released on bail. Soon after their release, Officer Murphy fell to the ground with convulsions. As time passed, his condition worsened. Despite the efforts of doctors, Officer Murphy died the next day. Warrants for the Duering brothers, charging them with the death of Officer Murphy, were issued immediately. James Murphy was twenty-three years old and single at the time of his death.

PATROLMAN JOSEPH C. CLARK

May 22, 1871, Middle District
5 years and 1 month of service

Twenty-one days after Officer Joseph Clark was appointed to the Baltimore Police, he answered a call for help at a house located on the corner of Holliday and Centre Streets. The keeper of the house at 23 Centre Street, Mrs. Annie Riley, had closed the doors of the house and set out for help. Soon after, she came into contact with Officer Clark and asked him to calm a rowdy tenant named Frederick M. Kussey. Officer Clark climbed the dark stairs of the house to the second floor and confronted Kussey.

For weeks prior to this confrontation, Kussey had bragged that he would shoot the first "speckled pup" that confronted him. "Speckled pup" was a derogatory term he was known to have used when describing policemen. In the darkness of a crowded hallway at about half past ten, Officer Clark struck a match to shed some light. In the glow of the single match, Officer Clark ordered Kussey to "Come along quietly." Kussey ordered one of the girls to go downstairs and get his hat. As she made her way down the steps, the twenty-three-year-old Kussey was true to his word: he withdrew a Colt seven-shot pistol and without warning fired three times. The shots shattered the quiet and struck Officer Clark in the mouth, cheek, and head, causing instant death. Kussey ran out onto Holliday Street and disappeared into the night.

After the shooting, as officers searched for him, Kussey wandered the streets before making his way to a bar at the corner of St. Paul and Fayette. There, after drinking for some time, he told the bartender, a Mr. Johnson, that he had shot a policeman and wanted to borrow money to rent a room at the Mansion House to avoid capture. Johnson found Officer Bradley and reported Kussey's location. Bradley enlisted the help of Officers McGuire and Chew. The three burst through the Mansion House door and arrested Kussey, still in possession of the pistol he had used.

Over two hundred officers from all four districts attended the funeral for Officer Clark. After the service, his body was taken from his home at 172 Harford Road and interred in the cemetery on the corner of Eager and Valley Streets. At the time of his death, Joseph Clark was fifty years old and was survived by his wife, nine children, and many grandchildren. Because his family had no means to provide for themselves, the city council introduced legislation to provide for the widows of fallen police officers and firefighters.

Detective John H. Richards

September 14, 1871
Criminal Investigation Division

Josiah Engler made the long trip into Baltimore from his rural home in Linwood, Maryland, to pick up supplies for his farm and family. After gathering what he needed in David Fontz's drug store at 116 Franklin Street, he loaded up and made the long trip home, only to discover on arriving that he had left his satchel with all of his business paperwork and money in the drug store. He returned to the store to reclaim his lost items, but by that time, Fontz had gone for the day. The only person left in the store was his clerk, twenty-five-year-old Daniel S. Miller. The satchel was gone as well. Engler went home empty-handed and suspicious of the young clerk. He wrote a letter to Fontz describing his satchel and hoping to enlist his aid in finding it. Fontz replied quickly, offering information that also implicated the store clerk.

Because of the importance of his satchel and its contents, Engler went to the Criminal Investigation offices of the Baltimore Police Department and recruited the help of Detective John Richards. Engler went over the facts of the case with Richards and the case against Daniel Miller became clear and strong. Detective Richards went alone to speak with Miller. As he walked up Franklin Street to the drug store he saw Miller on the sidewalk and called out to the young man, telling him why he had come to talk with him. On the street in front of many passersby, Miller pulled out a pistol loaded with buckshot and a ball round. On seeing the pistol, Detective Richards reached for his billy club to subdue Miller and take him into custody. Even though the department had begun issuing pistols to policemen in 1853, detectives often did not carry them. Miller shouted that Richards was not going to take him in and fired a shot that struck the detective in the arm then entered his chest. Richards fell to the ground.

The crowd of onlookers was stunned but soon gave chase. Miller tried to run but stopped when he realized that he would never outrun the men and women after him. He turned toward the crowd and pulled the trigger of his pistol again. This time there was only the snap of the pistol's hammer on an unresponsive charge. Confused, Miller frantically inspected his weapon, but as he looked the gun over, the buckshot exploded. In his haste to fix the malfunctioning pistol, Dennis Miller had shot himself in the head.

Detective Richards was taken to his friend's house at 88½ Mulberry Street, where he was expected to recover from his wound. Initial hope was soon replaced by despair, as he contracted an aggressive infection. Doctors did their best to alleviate his pain but realized that they could not prevent his inevitable death. Just after noon on September 14, after nearly twenty-four hours of delirium, John Richards died. He was forty-one years old, married with no children.

Patrolman John Christopher

August 23, 1872, Western District
1 year and 3 months service

The dust thrown up by two wagons rose in a blinding cloud as two teams thundered neck and neck down a path near the Catonsville Railway Park. The drivers cursed their horses and each other in a race that had ceased to be a friendly competition. The horses pulled hard as James Ford and James Dorsey cracked the reins against the animals' backs. The race had begun at Kelley's Woods in Catonsville and now reached the outskirts of Baltimore City. In a park near the Western District the men stopped and argued, drawing the attention of Officer John Christopher. As Officer Christopher neared, Ford and Dorsey began to fight. Using brute strength, Christopher separated the combatants and forced them back into their wagons.

To maintain peace, Officer Christopher climbed into Ford's wagon to ride with him as far as his destination. Despite Christopher's best efforts, the two drivers resumed their fight after only a short distance. Dorsey threw stones at Ford and warned him that if he bumped into his wagon again, he would shoot him. Fisticuffs resumed, and Dorsey pulled out a pistol. Officer Christopher saw it and gained control over the violent man by forcefully throwing him to the ground. The momentary separation was lost when Ford dove onto Dorsey and went for the gun. Before Officer Christopher could regain control over the men, the pistol fired. Even though Dorsey's anger focused on Ford, the bullet found its mark in the Christopher's stomach, causing a painful, fatal injury. Officer Christopher felt the deadly burn in his abdomen and fell to the ground.

John Christopher was immediately carried to the house of Justice Pilot and was given medical care by Dr. Worsham. Justice Pilot and John Young responded to the scene of the shooting and were able to arrest both men. Afterward, Officer Christopher was taken to his home at 14 South Fremont Street and cared for by Prof. J. H. Butler. His injuries were severe, and the medical professionals were unable to save his life. He lay in pain from the night of the shooting on August 19 until he died at approximately 3:30 in the afternoon on August 23, 1872.

Patrolman Charles W. Fisher

January 6, 1884, Eastern District
9 years and 8 months of service

In the late evening, the men of the Eastern District finished roll call and headed out into the biting cold to stand their tour of duty through a harsh winter night. Among them was Officer Charles Fisher, a proud father of five small children and a veteran of the American Civil War. He was a native of Germany who happened to be in Virginia at the start of the war, and so he served as a foot soldier wearing gray. At the end of the war he found himself in Baltimore, sometimes referred to as the northernmost southern city, and settled down to raise his family. By 1884 he had been on the force for more than nine years and knew his post well.

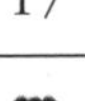

Fisher and his fellow officers knew that the night was going to be long and lonely. In such extreme cold, both criminals and law-abiding citizens usually stayed indoors and out of trouble. But the posts had to be manned, and that meant the men of the Baltimore Police Department walked. With his head bent down and his collar turned up, he walked his beat between Pratt and Fawn Streets, and between the Jones' Falls and High Streets. Just about every hour, Fisher came into contact with his side partners. At one o'clock in the morning, Officers Ahern and Fisher stood together in the middle of the street and talked. They spoke about the weather and their mutual relief that they would soon be headed home after a long tour of duty. Officer Fisher didn't complain about the cold but spoke of his eagerness to get back into his house at 109 S. Exeter Street. He told his fellow officer that he was going to make one more round of his post and call it an evening. They parted ways and Officer Ashen made his way back to the Middle District Station House. Thirty minutes later, Charles Fisher slipped and fell off a pier at the end of South Street. The harbor had long since been frozen over but the ice was not thick enough to prevent him from falling through.

Charles Butler was sleeping on the Eastern Shore steamboat docked there and heard the loud splash followed by someone yelling "My God!" He grabbed a lantern, alerted the vessel's private watchman, William Foster, and went to the ship's rail to peer into the darkness. Neither could see anything that signaled an emergency. Still concerned, Butler found a police officer and told him what he had heard. Soon after, Sergeant Reinhardt and two other officers from the Middle District responded to investigate. Insufficient light and horrible weather conditions made the rescue nearly impossible. They could barely make out the shape of an officer's cap and an espantoon lying on top of the ice. The number on the cap was 52. Sergeant Reinhardt notified the Eastern District by telephone, and Charles Fisher's side partners began a vain search of his post in the hopes that he was not under the ice.

By dawn, Charles Fisher's body was recovered and taken to the Eastern District. The investigation was brief. Initially it was thought that he might have been in a struggle with a suspect, because his espantoon was out of its holster, but later it was determined that Fisher had slipped and fallen off the pier accidentally. With the testimony of Charles Butler the investigation regarding the surrounding incident was quickly closed.

Patrolman
John T. Lloyd

July 4, 1889, Southern District
11 months of service

At half past one on the morning of July 4, 1889, Samuel Cooper, Edward Doyle, James Reynolds, and several others stood on the northeast corner of Light and West Streets outside a drug store. Their raised voices disrupted the night's peace and drew the attention of Officer John Lloyd, who was patrolling nearby. Officer Lloyd approached the group and ordered, "Do not make so much noise, the proprietor of the drug store will come down and complain."

With that, Samuel Cooper drew a pistol and fired in Officer Lloyd's direction. After the first shot, Cooper ran into the middle of the street, followed closely by Officer Lloyd, and continued to fire. In the street they struggled. Finally, with the third shot, Lloyd fell to the ground, struck in the abdomen and leg. Witnesses said that as soon as the officer fell, several of the men jumped on top of him trying to get him to relinquish his hold on Cooper. The ruckus and gunfire drew several more officers to the scene, where they arrested Cooper, Edward Doyle, and James Reynolds.

Officer John Lloyd, thirty years old and unmarried, lay in pain all day at his home until he succumbed to his injuries some fifteen hours later. Prior to his death, he was able to give an account of events to Justice Donovan, securing the successful prosecution of his attackers.

Patrolman Jacob Zapp

July 15, 1891, Southern District
18 years and 11 months of service

In a driving rain, Officer Jacob Zapp walked along the railroad tracks near Ostend and China Streets. The crashes of thunder masked the sound of Baltimore and Ohio Locomotive 634's backing as Officer Zapp walked with his head bowed against the downpour. He stepped onto the tracks in order to avoid a large puddle; witnesses stated that he did not see the train until it was too late. He instinctively raised his arm to protect himself just before he was struck.

Officer Zapp was killed instantly. People rushed to his aid but were unable to help in any way. His death was the first time in the history of the Baltimore Police Department that an officer, who suffered an accidental fatality, was recognized as having died in the line of duty. In the service of the public, members of the department are aware of the ever present danger of being attacked by criminals, and they do what they can to prevent those events. Equally possible is accidental death. By the very nature of the job, officers are more likely to find themselves in dangerous environments.

Officer Jacob Zapp was fifty-seven years old and had spent much of his life serving the citizens of Baltimore City.

Patrolman James T. Dunn

June 20, 1894, Central District
3 years and 6 months of service

Patrolman Michael Neary

June 20, 1894. Central District
16 years and 8 months of service

The Jones Falls is a beautiful, tranquil stream that winds through Baltimore. In the nineteenth century it was a popular place for young people to escape the summer's heat and socialize. One thing has remained the same: young people having a good time often become raucous and loud. This often generates citizens' complaints that have to be handled by the police. June 20, 1894, was a busy summer afternoon, and Officer Dunn, having already arrested one boy for swimming in the Jones Falls, was returning to his beat from the station. As he drew closer he could see even more people swimming and thrashing about in the water.

Officer Neary was at home when he saw the difficult time Officer Dunn was having. Even though he was off duty, Neary grabbed his overcoat, which identified him as a policeman, and set off to assist Officer Dunn in his duties. To get to the young men who were causing the disturbance, Dunn and Neary had to make a very difficult descent. They crossed over the Chase Street Bridge and made their way down a steep slope above the railroad, then walked several yards down the tracks toward a large gathering that had assembled to watch the policemen deal with the young men in the water. Tragically, what the onlookers next saw were the last few moments of the officers' lives.

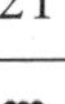

Dunn and Neary called to the boys in the water, two of whom voluntarily followed the officers' orders and made their way to the Chase Street Bridge by climbing up the opposite bank. The officers had to walk along the tracks in order to get back to street level and could not have seen the locomotive until it was too late. After departing Penn Station only a few minutes before, the Parkton Accommodation was gaining speed on its run. Witnesses reported the officers running for their lives, but because of their position on the tracks and the suddenness of the train's arrival, they had no chance. Both were stricken and killed instantly.

Officer Dunn had been married for three years and was the father of a six-month-old boy. Officer Neary had immigrated to the United States from Ireland when he was sixteen. He was married and left behind nine children, six sons and three daughters.

Patrolman John J. Dailey

October 17, 1895, Southern District
7 years and 4 months of service

Roger Dougherty, Patrick Kane, and John Diviney stood on the corner of Charles and Conway Streets making a disturbance shortly after midnight on August 26, 1895. The three had had frequent trouble with the police, and when they spotted Officer John Dailey walking on the opposite side of the street, they began to taunt and tease him as he patrolled his beat. Their behavior had its desired effect, and Officer Dailey crossed the street. When he attempted to place the three under arrest, a struggle began.

The barrage of feet and fists soon overwhelmed the outnumbered officer. His assailants threw him to the ground and continued to kick and beat him as he lay there, fading in and out of consciousness. The kicks and blows now found his head. The men ripped Dailey's club from his hands and used it against him. Then Roger Dougherty reached down and snatched the pistol from Dailey's holster. Unable to resist, Officer Dailey heard the gun discharge. He never felt the bullet enter his body and didn't know he had been shot until much later when he visited a doctor for a continuing pain in the small of his back. The scuffle drew the attention of Sergeants Straib and Evans and Patrolmen O'Hara, Whaley, and O'Conner, who arrived to see Dougherty fire the fatal shot. The three men were arrested and taken to the Southern District.

A doctor made the gruesome discovery of the bullet wound after a brief examination and soon determined the seriousness of the injury. Dailey was rushed to the University of Maryland Hospital. On being told that his wound was fatal, he insisted on going to his home at 117 West Clement Street. There, nearly two months later, Officer John Dailey died on October 17, 1895, leaving behind a wife and four children.

Patrolman Alonzo B. Bishop

August 29, 1899, Western District
13 years of service

Because of the nature of a port city, accidents were very common on the busy streets of Baltimore. Officer Bishop and Wagon

Driver William Smeak were on patrol in the Western District where Smeak had to steer his police patrol wagon amongst the heavy foot traffic and the constant rumble of streetcars. As they attempted to cross Freemont Avenue, Streetcar #556 of the Fremont Avenue Line struck their patrol wagon, and Officer Bishop was severely injured. Smeak and Bishop were responding to Call Box 23 at Poppleton and Pratt Streets for an officer who had made an arrest. Those who saw the streetcar strike the patrol wagon as it crossed the southbound tracks said it did so with such force that it threw the wagon against a telephone pole. Officer John Delaney witnessed the accident and quickly gained control of the horse and cart. He lifted both men into the wagon and took them to the University of Maryland Hospital. Smeak would be treated with serious but non-life threatening injuries.

For a long time, Officer Bishop lay in agony at the hospital. Doctors believed that if they could operate, they might save his life, but Bishop developed peritonitis, which made surgery impossible. In the early morning of August 29, 1899, Officer Bishop died. For the first time in the history of Baltimore City, an officer had lost his life as the result of a traffic accident. Officer Bishop was forty-two years old when he died and left a wife, two sons, John and Alonzo, both married, and a married daughter, Bessie Haugh.

The city would lose many more officers to traffic accidents. Across the nation, it is this hazardous daily activity that has become responsible for the majority of officers' fatalities in the line of duty. In the twenty-first century, the tracks that guided the streetcars are still visible and should serve as reminders not only of convenience, but of past dangers as well.

Patrolman Charles J. Donohue

May 20, 1902, Northeastern District
9 months of service

Police Officers care deeply about protecting those who cannot protect themselves. Often they are called to homes to help people in times of domestic troubles. Officer Charles Donohue went to the aid of a woman who was being assaulted by Charles Wilson, a violent man from Cockeysville, who had spent several terms in jail for various crimes. When Officer Donohue arrived at the house in the 1300 block of Whatcoat Street, he determined that he had to arrest Wilson and grabbed him by the arm.

Without warning, Wilson grabbed a beer bottle and struck Officer Donohue in the head. The blow disoriented Donohue, who struggled to gain his bearings. Officer Donohue drew his pistol in the defense of his own life, but, half-dazed, he had his revolver ripped from his hands. As Officer Donohue lay on the ground, unable to resist, Wilson stood over him and fired the officer's service weapon into his head, killing him instantly.

As Donohue lay dead on the floor, his killer fled the city. Eventually, Wilson would be captured and made to pay for his crimes. Officers know that in every situation a weapon is involved, their own. Unfortunately, criminals also know that a weapon is always within reach if the attack on an officer is fast, unexpected, and brutal enough. Several more officers in the city's history would lose their lives as a result of being attacked and killed with their own weapons. Their deaths must serve as loud reminders to all officers, of the ever-present dangers of police work.

PATROLMAN GEORGE C. SAUER

April 18, 1915, Eastern District
17 years and 1 month of service

David "Kid" Bender and James "Slim" Miller kept a diary of their criminal exploits as they robbed their way through Cleveland, Cincinnati, New York, and Philadelphia. Armed with .38 caliber pistols, they stole what they could to support what they believed to be the lifestyle of gangsters. In such fashion they made their way to Baltimore, where they met up with Joseph Grose. One of their first victims was a gentleman by the name of Charles Budd. On the night of April 9, 1915, the three approached Budd, who found himself staring down the barrels of two pistols. To save his life, he quickly gave up his inscribed watch and all the money he had. With the loot from their latest score, Kid, Slim, and Joe found a saloon and started drinking.

In 1915, Highlandtown was part of Baltimore County, and the liquor laws were not well enforced. Bars stayed open until they saw fit to close. One of the most famous bars in that area was called The Club, located at the corner of Eighth and Lombard Streets. After hours of drinking, Bender, Miller, and Grose started a fight they were destined to lose. The owner of The Club refused to serve the three and forcibly removed them after they pulled out their pistols and threatened the staff and customers. Thrown into the street and pursued by several angry men from the bar, Bender, Miller, and Grose drew their pistols and opened fire, but unable to hold their weapons steady, they missed everyone. With no time to reload, they ran to what they thought was the safety of Baltimore City. Eventually, they were able to evade their pursuers in the maze of streets and alleyways.

Without the threat of the crowd, the three slowed to a walk and reloaded their weapons. Still drunk at nearly four o'clock in the morning, they began to shoot randomly at windows and any hapless citizen who happened to be out and about. They walked down the center of Baltimore Street at the east end of Patterson Park, shooting into the air. A short distance away, at the intersection of Baltimore and Milton Streets, stood Officer George Sauer, who had just reported for duty. On hearing the shots, he hailed a passing taxi and stood on the running board as the driver sped toward their source. As the taxi neared the intersection of Baltimore and Decker Streets, Sauer spotted the trio shooting into the air. He drew his own pistol and took aim as he jumped from the running boards, shouting for the men to stop. Officer Sauer chased after them and successfully cornered the three near the intersection of Baltimore and Hare Streets.

Bender wheeled around and fired a single shot. The ball punctured Sauer's abdomen. Despite his wound, Sauer seized Grose and wrestled him to the ground. Bleeding but still maintaining control of Grose, Sauer shot several times into the air as a signal for help. Citizens and other officers, including an off-duty park patrolmen named Joseph Jaskoliski, ran to the scene with their own pistols and fired at Bender and Miller, who were running eastbound through the odd-side alley of Baltimore Street off Decker. Once again, they managed to escape. Responding officers held onto Grose while others lifted the wounded Sauer into a taxi and sped toward St. Joseph's Hospital. While the fifty-five-year-old Sauer lay unconscious, Grose divulged the identity and whereabouts of Bender and Miller.

A team of officers made their way to the O'Hara Hotel in the

100 block of Liberty Street to arrest Bender and Miller. Sergeants Wortman and Kelly, with Patrolman Sedicum, had the proprietor of the hotel knock on the door. Bender opened it slightly to see who was knocking. As he did, the two sergeants rushed Bender and tackled him while Sedicum jumped onto Miller. Miller tried to reach the pistol he had stashed beneath his pillow, but before he could do so, the two were quickly subdued and arrested. The officers recovered the pistols and called for a wagon to take the men to the Eastern District Stationhouse. On the way, Bender and Miller boasted of their criminal adventures and expressed regret for not "finishing off" Officer Sauer. They told those who had arrested them that they, "ought to go home and kiss their families, as they were lucky cops. . . . If we had seen you first, you wouldn't have lived to tell about it."

Officer Sauer regained consciousness long enough to identify the two but his doctors considered him too weak to undergo surgery. He succumbed to his wounds on April 18, 1915, leaving behind a wife, three daughters, and a son.

Bender readily admitted that he had fired the fatal shot. He and Miller were convicted of the officer's murder, as well as the robbery of Charles Budd. Grose was convicted of Budd's robbery as well but escaped being charged with murder. On December 30, 1915, Judge Carroll T. Bond sentenced Bender and Miller to eighteen years in prison, the longest term allowed at that time. In his official decision, Judge Bond described the two men as the worst criminals he had seen. He went on to say that Bender appeared "intense, strong willed, indifferent to the lives of others and likely to kill with something like pleasure."

Because of this particularly tragic incident, Mayor William Preston revived what he described as his "Borough Plan" and announced plans to annex Highlandtown and Canton into the city.

Patrolman John Lanahan

July 3, 1919, Central District
18 years and 7 months of service

Officer John Lanahan clearly enjoyed his profession, was highly regarded by his fellow officers, and was often described as one of the most efficient turnkeys in the department. After spending nearly twelve years on the street, he became the Central District Turnkey. For seven years he worked as a turnkey and took pride in treating those he booked with respect and dignity. His job was to take those who had been arrested, search them, book them, and keep them in a cell until they were able to see the court commissioner. Prisoners knew him for his kindness, and he made every effort to keep them in good spirits despite their unfortunate situation.

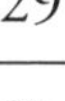

The morning of July 3, 1919, boded no differently for Officer Lanahan. He was on duty and helping to book a prisoner whom Officers Crass and Traupe had arrested for burglary. Frank Wozniak had been caught trying to pawn watches and jewelry he had stolen from the offices of the American Railway Express Company. During the walk to the station, Wozniak had made no attempts to resist the officers or flee from capture. In the station house, Lieutenant Klinfelter called to Turnkey Lanahan to begin the search of Wozniak's possessions. Lanahan approached the prisoner in his usual jovial and sympathetic way.

"Come, my boy, let me see what you've got," he said as he began to pat down Mr. Wozniak. Wozniak suddenly backed away, drew a pistol from his right pocket, and fired twice. The first shot struck

Officer Lanahan in the chest, piercing his heart. The second went wild. Before Wozniak could fire again, seven officers who had witnessed the event tackled him, wrestled the gun away and gained control. They found a second pistol in another of Wozniak's pockets as well as twenty more bullets.

Officers could not get their comrade to Mercy Hospital quickly enough, and John Lanahan was pronounced dead on his arrival by Dr. Eustace H. Allen of the Mercy surgical staff. Officer Lanahan left a wife, Mary Lanahan, two sons who served in the U.S. Armed Forces, and two daughters.

Patrolman Frank L. Latham

March 2, 1924, Eastern District
1 year and 8 months of service

Leon Schmidt and his wife, Agnes, quarreled constantly. Their marriage was desperate, and it did not help that Leon's mother, who lived with them, made no attempt to mask her disdain for her son's wife. Their fights were always intense, and on February 29, 1924, Leon's mother, eighty-one-year-old Annie, did her best to drive Agnes from the house. On this day, the threats Leon made against Agnes were serious, and she legitimately feared for her life as he chased her into the street. In order to preserve her own life and the life of her children, Agnes called for the police.

Officer Frank Latham answered the call at 511 South Collington Avenue. His course of action was clear. He had to arrest Leon to ensure the safety of Agnes and her children. Domestic violence is often unpredictable, and the responding officer's safety is in absolute jeopardy on each and every call. Whenever possible, several officers are dispatched to the scenes of family trouble because the situations are often unpredictable and can carry serious consequences. But on this day, Officer Latham was the first to arrive, and he was alone. The tension within the household had reached the breaking point. Several people were shouting, adding to the confusion. Officer Latham made his way toward Leon to arrest him, but as he drew near, Leon made up his mind that he was not going to jail. His anger manifested itself in senseless violence. He picked up his pistol and fired several shots, striking Officer Latham twice in the body.

The forty-year-old Schmidt grabbed what he could, went to his brother Walter's house for food and clothing, and fled to Carteret, New Jersey, knowing that if he were captured he would face the most extreme penalty. Detectives, convinced they could find him by interrogating his brother, questioned Walter Schmidt, who told them what they needed to know. A detachment of officers made its way to the small town twelve miles west of Newark. As Leon attempted to hide, Frank Latham died on a hospital bed in the Johns Hopkins Hospital on March 2, at the age of thirty-five, with his wife Ethel by his side. Now facing murder charges, Leon was arrested and taken back to Baltimore. Eventually, he was tried and sentenced to life in prison without parole. In a unique twist, Annie Schmidt, Leon's mother, faced charges of assault as well, on the grounds that Officer Latham's death could have been avoided if Leon's mother had not instigated the quarrel.

Patrolman Charles S. Frank

June 20, 1924, Southern District
7 months of service

The small, bushy haired man stared up at the judge with clear blue eyes and uttered the words "Not guilty." The blood of the officers who attended the hearing ran cold at this blatant lie. Fresh in the minds of the members of the Baltimore City Police Department was the loss of Officer Frank Latham, gunned down four months earlier under similar circumstances. The frustration of losing a close friend made the scene hard to bear. The little man stood there in a dirty brown coat and trousers with two days' growth on his face and denied the charges of first-degree murder.

Officer Charles Frank had gone to the house of Mr. and Mrs. Harry Jones at 1619 Marshall Street to stop a domestic quarrel. When he arrived Mrs. Jones met him in the street. She was hysterical and Officer Frank did his best to calm her. Without coherent information, he could not decipher what she needed. He did his best to get her back into the house so her neighbors would not scrutinize her troubles. Before they were both through the front door, Harry Jones slammed it shut, with Officer Frank still outside. As Frank pounded on the wooden door to get Jones to open up, bullets ripped through it and struck the officer in the stomach and chest. Confused and mortally wounded, Officer Frank stumbled into the yard and fired his pistol into the air to draw the attention of his fellow officers. A short distance away, Patrolman McCloakey heard the shots, came running, and arrested Jones on the scene. Hours later, at South Baltimore General Hospital, Officer Frank made a final deposition, naming Jones as his killer.

With all of this evidence facing him, including the testimony of his own wife as witness, he nevertheless stood before the bench and proclaimed his innocence. At the time of his death, Officer Frank was thirty-three years old and single.

Patrolman George D. Hart

January 1, 1925, Northern District, Motors Unit, 6 months of service

On November 16, 1924, a beautiful fall day, Officer George Hart steered his departmental motorcycle through the Northern District along the tree-lined streets of University Parkway near the Johns Hopkins University. A member of the Baltimore City Police Department for barely six months, he delighted in riding the motorcycle. Unfortunately a motorcycle is one of the most dangerous modes of transportation to operate on busy city streets, because other motorists often overlook them. Whether because of their small size or the fact that they are easily hidden by traffic, they are often unseen and therefore frequently involved in accidents.

On this day, a careless driver turned in front of Officer Hart at the intersection of University Parkway and North Charles Street, causing the fatal collision. Hart's wife Bessie would join him at Union Memorial Hospital, where on New Year's Day, 1925, he succumbed to his injuries. Officer Hart was the first Baltimore officer to lose his life as the result of a motorcycle accident. While his passing was a staggering blow to the entire department, as is every officer's death, that pain would reappear again later that same year, under similar circumstances.

Patrolman Roy L. Mitchell

November 1, 1925, Traffic Division, Motors Unit, 1 year and 4 months of service

On the afternoon of October 28, 1925, Patrolman Roy Mitchell climbed aboard his motorcycle, turned on his siren and red light, and tried to catch a driver roaring down Reisterstown Road. Winding into and through the city from rural Baltimore County, this busy thoroughfare has served as the major route for many who make their way into and out of Baltimore. As the twenty-eight-year-old patrolman on motorcycle number 280 weaved through traffic in his attempt to overtake the motorist, he was nevertheless careful to avoid pedestrians and cross traffic.

Officer Mitchell approached the intersection of Amos Avenue and Reisterstown Road just as John Cooley was driving his Dodge coupe north on the same stretch of Reisterstown Road. The two machines collided in the middle of the intersection and the motorcycle was crushed into the front of the oncoming car. Patrolman Mitchell flew into the air. After only a moment's hesitation, Cooley stepped on the gas pedal and raced away from the scene. Witnesses to the horrible sight were managed to record "7683" from Cooley's Maryland license plate. A citizen named J. G. Weisner, who watched the crash, rushed to the wounded officer's side.

Weisner placed the injured Mitchell in the back seat of his car and raced to the police sub-station at the corner of Reisterstown Road and Rogers Avenue, where Patrolman Isaac Miller called for medics. When the ambulance crew arrived they did their best to care for the massive head injuries and took the man to Maryland General Hospital. Dr. Kroll was able to stabilize the mortally wounded Mitchell. The next day, October 29, Lieutenant Charles Wilhelm, Sergeant Howard Gray, and Patrolman Frederick Knoerlein arrested Cooley. After posting a $1,000 bail, Cooley was released, charged with failing to give the right-of-way and failing to stop after an accident. Three days later, the charge of manslaughter was added when Patrolman Mitchell died from injuries sustained in the crash. Roy Mitchell was survived by his wife, Elizabeth.

Patrolman Webster E. Schuman

June 29, 1926, Northwestern District
3 years and 7 months of service

Station Clerk Thomas J. Dillon

July 12, 1926, Northwestern District
14 years and 4 months of service

On June 29, 1926, Rex Moore, the telephone operator for the Northwestern District, received frantic calls from citizens in the 600 block of West Lafayette and surrounding neighborhoods that a crazed man was wreaking havoc and shooting at people indiscriminately. Just before terrorizing his neighborhood, Vanie Lee, a discharged mental patient from Bay View Hospital, had become involved in a fight in a lunchroom near the intersection of Argyle and Lafayette. Arthur Redding, the owner of the lunchroom, confronted Lee, tried to calm him, and was shot in the neck for his trouble. After this initial shooting, eight others would be wounded, including four patrolmen and a police clerk.

Lee fled the lunchroom and made his way to his home at 635 West Lafayette, where he retrieved a rifle and another pistol. He then sat on his front steps with his weapons, lit a cigar, and smoked as he casually fired in the direction of passersby. As police officers do, Officers Webster E. Schuman, Ignatius Benesch, Howard L. Collins, Police Chauffeur Leroy E. Lentz, and Station Clerk Thomas J. Dillon made their way to Lee's house to deal with a deadly situation, while many others ran away. When they arrived they found that Lee had shot three citizens, two of them children: William H. Kammerer, who owned a drug store, sixteen-year-old Calvin Howard, and eleven-year-old Mildred Duncan.

Seeking a position of advantage, Officer Schuman sought cover in a grocery store across the street from the gunman. Lee took aim with his rifle and sent a round crashing through the plate glass of the store. The round found its way into the officer's mouth, mortally wounding him. The other officers saw their partner fall and set about to rescue him and provide aid. Station Clerk Dillon ran as fast as he could to get to the side of his wounded friend. Before he could reach the grocery store, the deranged gunman felled him with another shot from his rifle.

The other officers eventually gunned down Lee, but the damage was done. The two wounded men were taken to Colonial Hospital, where later that day Officer Schuman succumbed to his injuries. Police Commissioner Charles D. Gaither praised the courage of all the members of the department involved in this horrible event. "The patrolmen did everything possible under the circumstances. It is especially unfortunate that Mr. Dillon was shot, since he was unprepared for such action. Mr. Dillon volunteered when the call for reserves went out." During his time of service, all employees of the Department were considered to have police powers and although not usually called upon to help in such disastrous circumstances, Station Clerk Dillon would do all he could to help his fellow officers. He would lie in pain for nearly two weeks before he finally died from his wound on July 12, 1926.

Patrolman William F. Doehler

August 5, 1927, Northwestern District
7 years and 11 months of service

The young boys and girls of the Kornerstone Kindergarten in the northwest corner of the city wanted to make a difference. The plight of a blinded veteran tugged at their heartstrings, and they wanted to raise money by selling flowers to help the blind and financially strapped old soldier. With good intentions their only available currency, they sought help in the initial purchase of flowers. Without hesitation Officer William Doehler reached deep into his pockets and bought hundreds of tulips. Because of his generosity, the children went on to raise substantially more money and aided a man who had sacrificed much in the defense of his country. Officer Doehler was known in his community as a person who cared deeply about his neighbors and treated everyone, including the criminals he arrested, with dignity and respect.

In a pawnshop near the corner of Pennsylvania Avenue and Biddle Street a young man appeared unusually nervous as he tried to dispose of a stolen watch on August 5, 1927. The man, David L. Perry, moved about the shop nervously, hoping that he would receive cash for his stolen item. The shop owner recognized the signs of criminal behavior and notified the authorities. Officer Doehler responded to the shop, pieced together the facts, and decided to arrest Perry. The two men walked to a nearby call box and Officer Doehler called for a wagon to take Perry to the station for booking on charges of theft and burglary. The spectre of imminent imprisonment overwhelmed Perry, who determined to escape. Rather than breaking free and running, he made the decision to violently take another man's life. At that time the guiding rule of the police department was that a suspect was not searched prior to his arrival at the station house. Perry grabbed a pistol he had concealed in a pocket and fired a shot point blank into Officer Doehler's chest.

David Perry had just killed a man the northwest Baltimore community held near and dear to its heart. He knew he had little chance of escape but did his best, hiding in vacant houses and seeking refuge with people he thought he could trust. In the end he was caught, and, instead of the simple charges of theft and burglary, he had to answer for the crime of murder. In a newspaper article describing the community's outrage, a single printed picture evoked the strongest emotion. Officer William Doehler, in full uniform, stood amidst dozens of school children, all surrounded by tulips in full bloom. In an attempt to show its appreciation for the officer's dedication to the neighborhood, the *News-American* began a collection to support his widow and two children. Displaying a photograph of Officer Doehler's family in front of their home at 1838 West Mulberry Street the *News-American* declared: "This young officer gave his life for Baltimore's protection, for yours and your family's. Yesterday, they buried him . . . and so The News has started a fund for the family of this brave policeman, and is asking you to contribute."

Sergeant George M. J. May

February 12, 1928, Southern District
17 years and 9 months of service

As police use of automobiles increased, the risk of serious injury and death due to motor vehicle accidents kept pace. Although motorcycles were prevalent for a time because of their maneuverability and ease of operation, automobiles offered numerous advantages. They served as a type of "rolling office" for officers and as a sign of the police department making strides to modernize. With all of its advantages, the automobile quickly became an integral part of policing.

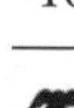

Automobiles have one distinct disadvantage on city streets, and that disadvantage would contribute to the death of Sergeant George May on the night of February 12, 1928. On the Hanover Street Bridge, Sergeant May was attempting to turn his vehicle around to check on Patrolman John Peters who was stationed at a police booth there when the Curtis Bay streetcar, unable to stop in time, broadsided his patrol car. This initial collision began an unexpected chain reaction.

Patrolman Peters witnessed the crash and rushed to his sergeant's aid, but he never made it. As he ran across Hanover Street, a delivery truck driven by John Fuchs struck him. May and Peters were transported to South Baltimore General Hospital. Patrolman Peters was treated for a broken leg; Sergeant May died from head injuries.

The Baltimore City Police Department had lost officers to traffic accidents prior to Sergeant May's passing, primarily officers assigned to motorcycle patrol. He was the first of many officers in the department's history to die in an automobile accident.

Detective Sergeant Joseph F. Carroll

November 19, 1928, Criminal Investigation Division, 21 years and 4 months of service

The young clerk, John McNabe, of the Commercial Hotel in the 700 block of East Baltimore Street did his best to appear casual as he registered the man standing in front of him. McNabe handed him the keys to Room #43 and telephoned the Detective Division. He reported that a man fitting the description detectives had given him earlier had just checked in.

Detectives had begun to circulate the description of a man wanted for many acts of violence in New York City, including the shooting of Patrolman George B. Wilson of the New York Police Department, as part of an effort that extended up and down the East Coast. Their target was a Danish man who went by the name Elmin Persson. Keeping the safety of the public in mind, the detectives thought it best not to tell the hotel clerks exactly what the various people were wanted for. When McNabe called he told detectives that a man wanted for "non-support or something" had just registered. Detective Sergeant Frederick W. Carroll, who had just reported to work that day, received the call and made his way alone to the hotel. Persson did his best to conceal his identity by using identification he had taken in an earlier robbery from a man named Peterson.

After several minutes of questioning, Sergeant Carroll decided that the man who called himself "Peterson," was the man that police were hunting for. Sergeant Carroll ordered him to get dressed and go to the headquarters building for more questioning. Persson took the overcoat hanging from the hotel room door and put it on. In the pocket was a pistol. As he dressed, the two men joked. Their conversation was lighthearted as they walked to the station. Persson's mind began to race.

Persson, who had come to New York aboard a Danish ship, had served in the Danish Marine Corps under his true name of Karl Jensen. While his ship was in port, he had deserted and disappeared into the city. He was already on the run from a heinous crime committed in his native country and thought that New York was the perfect place to avoid detection. Danish authorities were determined to find him and charge him with a brutal attack on a young girl.

Life soon prooved to be no easier in New York. After an unsuccessful attempt at boxing under the name of Battling Karl, he had acquired a gun and begun a spree of armed robberies. His robberies grew riskier as he became greedier and changed his name yet again. Calling himself Henry Peterson, he had entered a grocery store in Brooklyn, threatened the cashiers and helpless citizens with a gun, and made off with a large sum of money. Patrolman George B. Wilson confronted him at the front door, and gunfire erupted. Patrolman Wilson fell to the ground with serious injuries. With attempted murder now over his head, Jensen fled the city. He made his way to Philadelphia and continued to steal. For whatever reason, he traveled to Baltimore on the night of November 18, 1928, and registered in the Commercial Hotel under the name of Peterson.

Sgt. Frederick Carroll walked Jensen to the station with no knowledge of just how desperate this man was. It was still the written policy that, "Members of the force shall not search or act as witnesses to the searching of any person in any place other than the station house or headquarters, unless such search be made for dangerous or deadly weapons suspected to be upon the person of the prisoner." Therefore, Sergeant Carroll did not discover the pistol Jensen was carrying. In front of the headquarters building, Sergeant Carroll's fellow officers, including Patrolman Elmer O'Grady, leaned out of the window to watch as the two men walked inside. At that moment, Jensen decided to escape or die trying. He drew the gun from his coat and demanded that Sergeant Carroll give up his weapon and let him escape.

The officers reacted immediately. Sergeant Carroll grabbed at the assailant's weapon and the two began to wrestle. O'Grady ran from the building at a full sprint to help his fellow officer. Jensen pushed off of Fred Carroll and shot at O'Grady. Just as those first bullets flew, Sgt. Joseph Carroll and Patrolman Marts drove up to the scene in a patrol car. Sgt. Joseph Carroll was barely out of the car when Jensen shot him. Joseph Carroll staggered and fell in the street. Eventually, Jensen was rendered helpless but still alive from the barrage of police gunfire. Sgt. Joseph Carroll lay dead and Sgt. Frederick Carroll was seriously injured.

On his deathbed, Jensen made a full confession of his armed robberies and the shooting of three policemen, still using the name of Henry Peterson. He would die without admitting to the attack on the young girl in his native Denmark. In his confession, Jensen said, "When he mentioned the name of Peterson I knew what happened in New York, so I knew what they wanted me for." At the time of his arrest he knew that he would fight to the death to get away. "I had made it in my mind I would rather be shot than taken alive; that is the reason I did it, because I made up my mind I would not be taken alive."

"Sergeant Joe" as his fellow officers affectionately called him, was laid to rest on November 20, 1928, with hundreds of officers in attendance. A large detachment of New York officers was present to show their support. A special bond formed during this case between the members of the Baltimore and New York Police Departments as a result of this tragic circumstance, and that bond has strengthened and expanded to include all law enforcement officers, regardless of jurisdiction.

Patrolman John P. Burns

January 7, 1931, Northwestern District
10 years of service

On the afternoon of January 6, 1931, Patrolman Burns and Sgt. Alfred Plitt went to Willie Smith's house in the 500 block of St. Mary Street in response to a citizen's complaint of a disorderly person. When they arrived, they entered, with Burns in the lead. Before a word was spoken, Smith came down the stairs with a pistol in each hand, firing as he descended. Burns was immediately struck and fell to the ground. His breaths were short and shallow as the blood left his body. In the aftermath of the shooting, he lay in a pool of his own blood with sections of his uniform torn off and his badge ripped from his chest. The bullet had lodged close to his heart. Plitt engaged Smith in a close hand-to-hand battle. Drunk and out of control, Smith overpowered Sergeant Plitt and struck him in the head with the butt of a pistol, then ran from the house.

Sergeant Plitt was doing his best to run after Smith despite having been beaten severely. His vision was blurry from the blow to his head, and his walk was barely a stagger. Unable to run, he made his way out of the house and fell to the concrete sidewalk. Rising on one elbow, he emptied his revolver at Smith as he ran. Fortunately, one of Baltimore's brave citizens witnessed the event. Edward McIntyre, an employee of the Gas and Electric Company and close relative to several officers, stopped his van and went to the aid of the wounded sergeant. At the same time, another citizen, W. R. Kratz, stopped his automobile and helped McIntyre load Sergeant Plitt into another for transport to a hospital. Sergeant Plitt leaned against the car and reloaded his pistol. Despite his condition, he insisted on continuing the chase.

McIntyre supported him. They continued after Smith and cornered him in a basement entry in the 500 block of Orchard Street. McIntyre took Plitt's revolver and made his way to Smith's hiding place. Plitt's head wound grew worse, and he was unable to help in the capture of the criminal. Smith hid and waited, breathing hard from his sprint to temporary freedom. He put one of his pistols down on the concrete ledge as he reloaded the other. By this time, backup had arrived, and McIntyre crept toward Smith as quietly as he could with Patrolman David Weed by his side. McIntyre snatched Smith's pistol as it lay on the ledge, and the gun battle raged. Weed and McIntyre fired simultaneously, riddling Smith with bullets. Willie Smith died instantly.

Patrolman John Burns was barely alive when he arrived at University Hospital. His wife Margaret was brought to the hospital and was overcome with grief. She collapsed and had to be admitted for treatment. A request for suitable blood donors was made and over five hundred police volunteered their services. Despite this overwhelming support, Patrolman Burns succumbed to his wound on January 7, 1931, his wife by his side. John Burns's death was hardest for his young daughter Charlotte. "Little Charlotte, too young to realize that the hand of death forever had taken the one she loved and admired, continually asked; 'When will Daddy be home?'"

Patrolman William A. Bell

January 2, 1932, Northwestern District
23 years and 3 months of service

Shortly before nine o'clock in the evening on January 2, 1932, Patrolmen William Bell and William Sempeck crept along quietly on the third floor of an apartment building at 1709 Madison Avenue. Patrolman Bell had just received information from a confidential informant about the location of a violent felon who was wanted on many warrants, including one for a robbery he committed in the 300 block of East 25th Street. This felon, Wilbur Wright, was known for always carrying at least two pistols. The two officers took positions next to the apartment doors. Sempeck took one look at his partner and made his way into the darkened apartment. Even though they did their best to be unnoticed, Wright knew they were there. When Sempeck took his first steps into the apartment, Wright burst through the door that Bell was standing behind. Wright had the element of surprise on his side and shot Bell three times.

Sempeck heard the shots and ran into the hallway in time to catch Bell as he fell to the floor. "I tried to catch Bell as he was falling. Then I laid him on the floor and started after Wright, who was running down the stairs," said Sempeck. By the time Sempeck was able to give chase, Wright had a substantial lead. After a short pursuit, Sempeck knew he would be unable to catch the murderer and returned to Bell's side. By that time, his partner was dead. Within minutes, every police district had been notified and scores of officers and detectives began a search of the entire city. Inside the apartment that Wright had been using as his hideout, officers found two more guns, a .45 caliber automatic and a .45 caliber army revolver. Wright hailed a taxi the following morning and made his escape, heading for Washington D.C.

Detectives charged with tracking the murderer quickly found that Willie Wright made a living by taking from others. He had spent years in the penitentiary for many different crimes, including larceny, burglary, purse snatching, and carrying concealed weapons. The neighborhood surrounding the 1700 block of Madison Avenue was in constant fear of this violent felon. Despite his years of punishment, he continued to commit crime after crime. Wilbur Wright had now become a murderer and had run to where he thought he was safe. A task force led by Lt. Nicholas Gatch, which included Detectives John C. Dalglish and Carlton Galley, went to the capital, tracking him to an apartment at 1029 Fourth Street, in the Northwest section of the city. The detectives hid in the shadows of the apartment building waiting to trap their quarry. In the early afternoon of January 3, 1932, Wright looked cautiously over his shoulder as he made his way to his safe house. When he entered the front door, the detectives jumped from their hiding places and pressed their pistols into his side. They found the revolver he had used against Patrolman Bell, still containing the three empty shells in the cylinder.

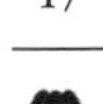

Arrested and charged with the murder of a policeman, Wilbur Wright sat in his cell at the Northwestern District back in Baltimore, laughing at the comics section of the local newspaper. He never expressed the slightest bit of remorse for killing the fifty-two-year-old man who had spent more than twenty-three years of his life in the service of the citizens of Baltimore. At the time of his death, William Bell was unmarried and survived only by his mother Emma.

Patrolman Thomas F. Steinacker

October 4, 1932, Southwestern District
44 years and 4 months of service

The memo written by the Southwestern District Commander, Capt. John Robinson, was submitted to the Chief Inspector with the simple subject title, "Death of Officer Thomas F. Steinacker." In a two-sentence report, the forty-four-year career of a man was officially ended. "Officer Thomas F. Steinacker of this district died at 3:30 P.M. He is a member of the Insurance." During his career, Thomas Steinacker had had a front seat to history. He had watched Baltimore Town grow into Baltimore City; he had seen the city line extend itself in all directions and a proud metropolis take shape. Modern electric streetcars carried loads of people to and from their destinations and new docks allowed the largest of vessels to weigh anchor in one of the most important ports on the East Coast. In 1932 he saw the beginnings of motorized police patrol with the use of "Scout Cars." These cars helped officers respond when timeliness was of the utmost importance.

With all of the technological advances available to the department, most officers still walked a foot post, answering calls for service dispatched by desk sergeants to call boxes mounted on the corners. Sometimes officers got a quick assist by jumping onto passing street cars, but always they were mindful to respond when the call box light flashed.

On September 29, 1932, in the middle of the morning, Patrolman Steinacker, who had turned seventy years old in his forty-fourth year of policing and was still in love with his job, was walking his post near the intersection of Willard Street and Frederick Avenue only blocks from his home. He came to a busy Frederick Avenue and took his chance crossing in front of a truck driven by Paul Simpson of Newmarket, but he never made it. Simpson's truck hit Patrolman Steinacker with great force, throwing him through the air and into a passing streetcar owned by the United Railway and Electric Company. His body came to rest in the middle of the street, where he lay motionless with a fractured skull and other injuries. Several citizens stopped to help the fallen officer and rushed him to nearby St. Agnes Hospital for treatment, but the injuries were beyond a doctor's help. He held onto life until October 4, 1932. His wife Emma was given a pension to assist her with bills and expenses that she would now face alone. Thomas and his fellow officers had been given the option to prepare for this situation by joining what was popularly called "The Insurance," a fund designed to help the spouses and children of officers killed in the line of duty. In forty-four years of service, the Insurance helped the families of more than twenty officers.

Patrolman John R. J. Block

April 21, 1933, Southern District
12 years and 6 months of service

Kenneth Lewis, Troy Boyd, and a third man who would never be identified or brought to justice, had planned for days to hold up bus drivers working for the United Bus Company. When the hour came, they armed themselves with several pistols and a rifle and put their plan in motion. Lying in wait at the bus terminal, they watched William Hoffmaster steer his bus into its parking space and prepare to go home for the evening. Two of them crept toward Hoffmaster's bus and without warning stormed it and threatened him with guns. They took all of the money he had on his person and the fares he had collected during the day. As they robbed Hoffmaster, the third man made his way toward Lawrence Huster, another driver who was seated inside his bus.

Huster was forced at gunpoint into Hoffmaster's bus, where he was also robbed. The trio threatened the two men by saying if the bus drivers tried to alert anyone or defend themselves, they would be killed "deader than hell." The three then fled the scene, with much destruction to follow. They had not counted on the swift reaction from the Baltimore Police and soon found themselves the subject of a massive manhunt. Armed with a description of the car, officers began an intense search for the suspects. The three robbers decided it was best to escape by going south through the city toward Annapolis.

At the corner of Hanover and Jack Streets, Officer John Block observed the getaway vehicle with Florida tag 115-345. As Officer Block approached the car, Lewis and Boyd leapt out and began firing. Taken by surprise, Officer Block was unable to return fire. Backup arrived as the suspects sped away. Officer Block died soon afterward, while being treated at the South Baltimore General Hospital.

Police soon tracked down Kenneth Lewis at a farmhouse near Brushy Fork, West Virginia. Cornered, with no option but surrender, Lewis placed his gun to the side of his head and took his own life. Troy Boyd was later arrested and sentenced to eighteen years in jail for his part in the slaying of Officer Block.

Patrolman John Blank

February 11, 1934, Northeastern District
11 years and 2 months of service

Desperation and hopelessness pervaded America in the mid-1930s as the Great Depression tightened its grip. With the highest rate of unemployment in the country's history, violent crime skyrocketed. Gangs seemed to operate everywhere, smuggling liquor, holding up business owners, and taking advantage of vulnerable people. The Touhy Gang was one of the more violent groups that worked on a national scale. Originating in Chicago, this collection of criminals wasted no time in becoming one of the nation's most notorious gangs. Bold enough to kidnap a member of a rival gang, John "Jake the Barber" Factor, they began a countrywide tour of crime.

In North Carolina, the Touhy Gang made its largest heist. A mail truck loaded with cash, destined for area businesses, was brought to a sudden halt through a coordinated effort. As the truck traveled down a street in Charlotte, two automobiles cut it off and forced it to a sudden stop. Men seemed to emerge from everywhere, and one brandished a machine gun. Helpless to stop the robbers, the mailmen wisely followed their instructions. In doing so, they preserved their own lives. The Touhy Gang made off with $105,000. They split the money and did their best to evade the federal authorities hunting them. Several members of the gang made their way to Baltimore.

In addition to common crime, the work of gangs such as this one left police officers with their hands full, and Patrolman John Blank worked as hard as any. Blank patrolled his post on foot, made sure to check the businesses on his post frequently, and was known as a professional in the community. While making his way through his beat, he became suspicious when he spotted evidence that someone had broken into a major business. In the 1400 block of North Central Avenue, Patrolman Blank and fellow Patrolman William Atkinson were checking the H. L. Carpel Mayonnaise Plant by making sure all of the doors and windows were secure, when through a window Blank noticed that someone had moved the company's safe from the office onto the main factory floor. It was nearly midnight. Atkinson covered the front as Blank made his way to the rear of the plant. In the dark alley, Blank found a door near a garage and attempted to enter. His suspicions proved correct.

Not long before, members of the Touhy Gang had used explosives to open the safe and remove $1,120. Unknown to Blank as he stealthily made his way down the dark alley, he was moving toward a lookout hiding in the shadows. Finished with their crime, the two members of the gang inside the factory came to the open rear door, saw the patrolman, and shouted, "Look out, Mack!" The lookout raised a pistol and fired. John Blank fell to the ground dead from a bullet wound to the head. The three burglars ran down the alley out into Oliver Street and disappeared onto Eden Street. Patrolman Atkinson heard the shot and ran from the front of the factory to find his friend and partner dead. Investigation would eventually supply the physical descriptions of the killers, but police would not immediately connect the slaying to the Touhy Gang.

Officers felt the horrible loss of a brother, but had to continue their daily duties of fighting crime. With the thought of Patrolman Blank's death fresh in his mind, Sergeant Oscar Lusby made his way to the Northern District Station at Keswick and 34th Streets. On this cold winter day, Sergeant Lusby spotted an automobile parked at the corner of St. Paul and 33rd Street that matched the description of the Touhy Gang's car. Fortunately he was in plain clothes and could keep an eye out for the fugitives without arousing suspicion. The Northern District commander, Captain Joseph Wallace, assembled an arrest team in coordination with the Headquarters Detective Division. Lusby's and Wallace's quick thinking paid off.

As the police watched, Basil H. "The Owl" Banghart walked to the car and settled into the driver's seat. Captain Wallace approached the car with several patrolmen under his command and thrust a pistol into Banghart's face, capturing the gangster by surprise. The takedown was quick out of necessity. In order to catch all of the gang members they could, the officers knew they had to maintain a discreet surveillance. Through patience and effective use of police techniques, they eventually captured Isaac Costner, Jessie Touhy, the wife of "Tommy" Touhy, brother of the gang's leader, and May Davis. The four had rented rooms in an eight-story apartment building named Green Hall with the money stolen in the mail robbery. In their seventh-floor apartment police found two Thompson submachine guns, two repeating shotguns, one Winchester repeating rifle, three .45 caliber automatic pistols, one .38 caliber pistol, one loaded tear-gas pistol, one "regulation Mail Service pistol," a large cache of ammunition, and $12,500. Despite their arsenal, patrolmen of the Northern District arrested these dangerous criminals without firing a single shot. Eventually, the other members of the Touhy Gang, Ludwig "Dutch" Schmidt and Charles "Ice" Connor, were also arrested.

Detectives soon discovered that the Touhy Gang was responsible for the murder of Patrolman John Blank. With less than a year of service, the forty-four-year-old patrolman left a wife, Anna, behind. With a full contingent of police, a funeral was held at Blank's house at 132 South Clinton Street. On Thursday, February 15, at 10 A.M. the procession made its way to the Holy Redeemer Cemetery.

Patrolman John A. Stapf

November 2, 1934, Northwestern District
33 years and 7 months of service

Officer John A. Stapf had just finished talking to the officers who were going to relieve him from his post. Officers Stapf, John Schmidt, and Edward Burns stood at the call box on North Avenue under the Western Maryland Railway Bridge. As Officers Schmidt and Burns boarded an eastbound trolley car, Officer Stapf attempted to get across North Avenue quickly by running around the trolley as it stood waiting for passengers. In his haste he neglected to look for oncoming traffic.

In the westbound lanes he was struck by another trolley. The impact was so severe that it threw Officer Stapf back into the eastbound trolley his fellow officers had just boarded. Schmidt and Burns witnessed the accident and rushed to their friend's aid, but shortly afterward, Officer Stapf was pronounced dead from severe head injury at the West Baltimore General Hospital.

Officer Stapf was sixty-three years old at the time of his death and was survived by his wife, Katherine, sons George, William, John, and Garland, and daughters Lillian, Margarete, and Florence. He had served the citizens of Baltimore for nearly thirty-four years and had received numerous awards and citizen commendations.

Patrolman Henry Sudmeier

December 20, 1934, Northern District
9 years and 3 months of service

On the night of October 19, 1926, Officer Henry Sudmeier went into a dark church to investigate a burglary in progress. He turned on his flashlight and began a systematic search for the suspect in the Sacred Heart Catholic Church in Mount Washington. Soon after, his fellow officers arrived on scene to assist him. The backup officers also began their own search. They crept along in darkness, walking as quietly as they could, looking and listening for any signs of an intruder. One of the officers saw a faint light near the back of the church.

Focused on the light, they made their way to uncover what they thought was the suspect. With drawn pistols the officers took a position of advantage and waited to spring their trap. Officer Sudmeier never knew that his fellow officers were in the church and had not made his presence known. He silhouetted himself with his flashlight and one of his backup officers mistaking him for a burglar, took aim and fired. The bullet struck Officer Sudmeier's spinal cord, paralyzing him instantly.

For eight years, Officer Sudmeier received the best possible medical care at Mercy Hospital, but on December 20, 1934, he succumbed to his wounds. At the time of the shooting Officer Sudmeier had one and a half years of service. He was survived by his brother Wilbert, who became a Baltimore police officer in 1937.

Patrolman Max Hirsch

February 14, 1935, Southern District
6 years and 11 months of service

In the rear of 614 Light Street, Officer Hirsch found a garage door unsecured. An anonymous citizen had reported to police that a person had broken into the location and was attempting to steal property from within. Carefully, quietly, and thoroughly he began to check the interior of the building. Finding nothing on the first floor, he continued to the second floor of the garage. The footing was perilous and it required great skill to maintain his balance. As he walked along the edge overlooking the concrete first floor he suddenly confronted a man who was trying to conceal himself in the building to avoid detection.

The suspect startled Officer Hirsch in his attempt to escape. He ran down to the first floor and out the rear door, never to be seen again. As the officer gave chase he slipped and fell from the second floor to the unforgiving concrete below. In his day, Officer Hirsch and his partners had to be self-sufficient. They had to be physically and mentally competent enough to handle most police work without the help of others. It was not uncommon for officers to work an entire shift without seeing one another. Now Officer Hirsch lay helpless within the garage. None of his fellow officers knew where he was, what he had been doing, or that he had been severely injured. They did not look for him.

Not until approximately six o'clock in the morning, several hours after his fall, did Officer Hirsch manage to find help. He summoned the strength to make his way from the floor of the garage to the firehouse at the corner of Light and Montgomery Streets. Saying only "I fell," Officer Hirsch collapsed on the floor inside the fire station and fell into a coma. Several firemen offered to help and transported him quickly to the South Baltimore General Hospital, where doctors diagnosed him with a fractured skull but could not revive him. Later, Officer Hirsch succumbed to his injuries. The forty-one-year-old officer was survived by his wife.

Patrolman Arthur H. Malinofski

October 31, 1935, Northwestern District
9 years and 1 month of service

Around four o'clock on the morning of October 31, 1935, Officer Arthur Malinofski parked his patrol car in a lot just off Maine Avenue near Gwynn Oak Avenue. To safeguard nearby businesses, Officer Malinofski was making a routine check of the rear doors. Flashlight in hand, he walked quietly, pulling on doors to ensure that they were secure. Just yards away, Oscar Norfolk was breaking into one of those stores.

The flashlight's beam fell on Norfolk as he was attempted to pry open a door. Both Norfolk and Officer Malinofski reacted in surprise. Officer Malinofski reached for his gun, but he was slowed by the fact that he was holding his flashlight. Norfolk wheeled around and began shooting. The bullets struck Officer Malinofski, dropping him immediately. Drawn to the sound of gunfire, a milkman on his delivery rounds rushed to Officer Malinofski's aid as Norfolk fled the scene. He discovered the lifeless body of the officer just feet from his patrol car, with his flashlight still in his hand and his revolver secured in its holster.

Patrolmen Anthony Staylor and Henry Levinson apprehended Norfolk some time later. After being interrogated by Lieutenant Edward Hitzelberger, Norfolk was booked for the "assault and shooting" of Officer Malinofski. Commissioner Gaither commented on the shooting and praised the fallen officer. He spoke of how quickly the shooting had occurred and how unfortunate it was that a simple thing such as a flashlight had slowed his ability to defend himself.

Patrolman Leo Bacon

October 9, 1936, Traffic Division
8 years and 10 months of service

On February 26, 1932, Officer Bacon was coordinating the difficult task of maneuvering a semaphore house through traffic at the intersection of Eutaw and Saratoga Streets. He was a very capable officer who had performed this type of task many times before. Unfortunately, on this day the operator of the massive vehicle lost control and left Officer Bacon with a serious abdominal injury. It was later discovered that he had suffered significant damage to his kidneys. The injury continually aggravated him until he finally sought the attention of a doctor.

After initial treatment, Dr. A. J. Gillis made a diagnosis of epididymitis in the right side. He also found that Officer Bacon had a stone in the left kidney severe enough to warrant surgery. Dr. Gillis believed this condition was related to the accident and the injuries sustained that day.

As a result of complications following surgery, Officer Bacon died on October 9, 1936. The department declared that since the injury and surgery were a direct result of the accident in 1932, his passing was in the line of duty. Commissioner Charles D. Gaither and the department awarded Mrs. Bacon line-of-duty death benefits in January 1937.

Patrolman Carroll Hanley

October 29, 1936, Central District
21 years and 2 months of service

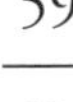

The Depression of the 1930s hit many people hard. As people looked for work, the short-staffed Baltimore City Police Department was overwhelmed with the job of protecting its citizens. Like most arms of government, the department was strapped for cash and forced to tighten its belt to make ends meet. On August 2, 1932, the men of the department agreed to a ten percent reduction in salary. On December 28, 1933, they agreed to another five percent reduction.

Despite these reductions in salary, Officer Carroll Hanley, like everyone else, worked hard. On the morning of October 29, 1936, he made a car stop in the unit block of North Avenue outside the Backus Chevrolet Company. The car lurched forward as the driver attempted to escape. In an attempt to maintain control of the situation Officer Hanley jumped onto the side running board. He held onto the vehicle as the driver sped through rush hour traffic, taking incredible risks and turning as sharply as possible in an effort to throw the officer off.

As the driver rounded the corner of East 20th Street and Hargrove Alley, several blocks away, Officer Hanley lost his hold and was thrown to the ground, where he lay with severe injuries in desperate need of help. Eventually, he was transported to Union Memorial Hospital too late to save his life. Even after the pay cuts that Officer Hanley and his fellow officers had agreed to in order to keep the department functioning effectively, he continued to serve his city and put his life on the line.

Patrolman John T. King, Jr.

December 28, 1936, Northeastern District
13 years and 8 months

Patrolman John King's personnel folder is stuffed with reports documenting acts of heroism and bravery. Among these official reports and forms is a handwritten letter from a grateful father. On Thursday, May 30, 1935, Mr. Harry Hallock put pen to paper to express his thanks to an officer who had made a difference in his life. What might have been a trivial matter for the officer had had a profound effect on Mr. Hallock.

It was an act that typified John King's character as a man and officer. He had come across a young girl, Hallock's daughter in need of help. As she was walking through the Mt. Royal Station of the B&O Railroad, she had fallen and cut herself on an exposed pipe. John scooped her up in his arms and carried her the entire distance to the hospital to receive care. Not only did he carry her the whole way, he stayed with the child while she was treated. When nurses and doctors were too busy, he found other caregivers who were not. Like all officers, John King faced danger every day. He chased down armed men in dark alleys and arrested some of the most violent criminals. But he was most proud of the letters from the thankful fathers of the people he helped.

A year and a half later, at forty minutes before midnight on December 27, 1936, Patrolman King crossed the intersection of Hoffman and Caroline Streets. The danger he faced was not pointing a weapon at him. No violent felon was trying to escape, nor was it anything for which he could have prepared. As he walked his beat, he was surprised by an automobile bearing down on him. The speed was too great and the patrolman was helpless to escape. The car, driven by William Higgins, slammed into the officer and threw him across the street.

Higgins and his passenger, John Donovan, panicked. They knew they were wrong, and they tried to cover up their negligence. As Patrolman King lay on a hospital bed in severe pain, attended by Dr. Francis Coleman, a number of his fellow officers gathered around him—Lt. Leo Kelly, Sgt. Edward Eben, and Patrolmen Albert Schultz, and Ernest Grimes. John Donovan approached the group and brazenly accused the severely injured officer of being drunk at the time of the accident. He then produced the broken neck of a whiskey bottle that he said he had found in the injured patrolman's coat pocket. As much as this angered them, King's friends had the presence of mind to examine his uniform and person to be sure that Donovan's claim had no merit. Reports filed by the doctor and fellow officers debunking the criminal's claim soon proved the lie. The coroner later agreed: Patrolman King had not been drunk; Higgins's gross negligence had led to the officer's death. Sadly, John's wife Margaret was by his side when he died, and to hear the disgusting lie.

Patrolman King had suffered fractures in each leg, internal injuries, abrasions, and shock. The doctors did what they could, but the injuries were greater than they could overcome. They tried several transfusions of blood, but the treatment was ineffective. On December 28, 1936, John King died. In order to help Mrs. King make ends meet, she was awarded a pension of twenty dollars per week from the Special Fund the department maintained.

PATROLMAN THOMAS J. BARLOW

December 31, 1937, Northeastern District
14 years of service

In the early morning hours of December 31, 1937, a young woman near the intersection of Belair Road and Pelham Avenue screamed for help. Officer Thomas Barlow heard the urgency in her voice and ran to her as fast as he could. With the streets nearly deserted, he raced across Belair Road to stop an assault in progress. As he focused on the struggle in front of him, he did not see a car traveling toward him.

Before he knew it, Officer Barlow was airborne, struck by a driver who had not seen him. Officer Barlow suffered severe internal injuries as well as fractures in both legs. Shortly afterward he was taken to the closest hospital, where he died. When this type of accidental death occurs, it greatly saddens all of the members of the department greatly.

Not only does it bring to mind the fact that this type of death is preventable, it also makes officers realize the many times that they have done exactly the same thing.

Chief Engineer Joseph E. Keene

November 1, 1938, Harbor Patrol
15 years and 10 months of service

Baltimore's history as a port city is a long and storied one, with its maritime roots extending deep into the days of this nation's beginnings. Because of the large amount of boat traffic and the efforts of criminals to take advantage of those who make their living on the open seas, officers have patrolled the harbor since the birth of the city. Joseph Keene served as an engineer whose primary responsibility was the maintenance and repair of the Harbor Patrol's watercraft. He was a highly skilled man who worked incessantly.

On the morning of October 24, 1938, he had taken on the task of repairing the troublesome motor of a boat docked at the foot of Wells Street. The job required that he run the engine as he worked on it. Before he could discover the malfunction causing the engine's problems, he began to feel dizzy and light-headed. He decided to leave the small, enclosed engine compartment and get some fresh air. His condition worsened as he made his way topside. His head continued to cloud and his dizziness gave way to confusion and disorientation. As he walked along the pier attempting to clear his head, he stumbled repeatedly. Soon after, he fell and lost consciousness.

Unknown to Chief Engineer Keene, the motor he was working on had two small holes in the exhaust that leaked carbon monoxide.

He died several days later as a result of carbon monoxide poisoning. During his time in service, all employees of the department, regardless of job title, were sworn members. As a result, Commissioner Robert F. Stanton awarded his wife Anna a full police pension for his death in the line of duty.

Patrolman William L. Ryan

June 13, 1940, Central District
19 years and 3 months of service

The Grace Hope and Mission cross hangs today in the unit block of South Gay Street. For many years the workers of the mission house have made great efforts to help those less fortunate. On the morning of June 13, 1940, beneath the mission's cross, a deranged man, Joseph Abata, held citizens at bay with a butcher's knife. As he wildly swung his weapon, Officer William Ryan did what the citizens asked of him. He closed the distance, doing his best to safeguard the lives of the people around him.

Officer Ryan's approach sent the violent man over the edge. Abata lunged and sank the blade deep into Officer Ryan's chest with one violent swing. The horrified crowd stood in shock as the enraged Abata struck again and again. Somehow Officer Ryan managed to fight off the attacker, who ran away. As Abata ran south on Gay Street, Officer Ryan fired twice, but in his condition he missed both times.

The crowd of witnesses, which included fire fighters and citizens, found the courage to chase after Joseph Abata and eventually capture him. Ryan was rushed to Mercy Hospital where he was pronounced dead on arrival. Abata was found not guilty by reason of insanity and was sent to Spring Grove Hospital.

Patrolman William J. Woodcock

June 13, 1943, Central District
19 years and 3 months of service

In the shadows of the Penitentiary, Ronald "the Maniac Bandit" Harris sat on the doorstep of a house in the 400 block of East Eager Street with three of his friends. Harris, Wesley Doxon, Amos Morey, and Lewis Crites were known to all of the patrolmen in the area as a constant source of trouble. In and out of jail, Harris started his criminal career in 1918 with crimes that included burglary, larceny, assault, carrying a deadly weapon, robbery, and shooting at police. At almost ten o'clock on a warm summer Saturday evening, Patrolman William Woodcock was called to the 1000 block of Brentwood and told by residents that Harris and his friends were harassing people in the neighborhood. Patrolman Woodcock set out to find the disorderly group.

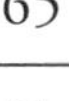

As the patrolman turned the corner, he found the four on Eager Street. After an exchange of words, Woodcock decided to arrest Harris for disturbing the peace and grabbed him by the belt. Woodcock began to walk Harris to the nearby call box to request a patrol wagon to take his arrest to the station. Without handcuffs, as police often were, patrolmen were vulnerable to attack. With the officer's hand tightly wrapped around the belt in the small of Harris's back, Harris suddenly spun around. His brutal attack caught Patrolman Woodcock by complete surprise. Harris landed several blows before the officer could defend himself.

When the attack began, May Blessing was watching from her window at 1004 Brentwood. Harris struck Patrolman Woodcock repeatedly in the head as he fell to the ground. Mrs. Blessing rushed to her phone and called the Central District to get help for the overwhelmed officer. When she returned to her window, she saw that Doxon, Morey, and Crites had joined Harris. Instead of fighting just to get away, the four beat the patrolman savagely, then fled before help arrived, leaving the semi-conscious patrolman for dead. Responding officers transported Patrolman Woodcock to the hospital where he faded in and out of consciousness. When Woodcock was lucid enough to speak, he told his commander, Captain Joseph Itzel, about the attack. He was able to name his attackers and describe the sequence of events. Early on the morning of June 13, 1943, Patrolman William Woodcock faded out of consciousness for the last time, and passed away. A detail of officers was formed and the manhunt began. The four were arrested after a brief and intense search.

Patrolman Woodcock was not simply a police officer. He was a loving husband and the father of two young men who were serving their country during World War II. He had suffered the pain of loss the previous fall, when his son, Charles Woodcock, had been killed in combat in the Pacific. An "Inspector's Funeral" was held for William Woodcock at his home, 329 South Fulton Avenue.

Patrolman William S. Knight

November 7, 1943, Northeastern District
7 years and 4 months of service

At ten minutes after 10 P.M. on November 7, 1943, someone began shooting wildly in the 1100 block of Rutland behind the East Molting Republican Club. Officer William Knight and his partner John Bianca responsed to the calls from concerned citizens and patrolled the area in search of the gunman. Thomas Toler, the shooter, soon made his whereabouts absolutely clear by firing a shot into the air. He then ran across Rutland in front of the two officers. Bianca bailed out of the car and chased the man as Knight drove his car around to Broadway to apprehend him as he came out of the alley.

Bianca soon lost sight of Toler and began to look for his partner heading toward Broadway. He heard the ominous sound of gunfire ahead of him near the intersection of Broadway and McDonough Street, knew that his partner needed him and sprinted to his side. What he found left him bewildered. William Knight was slumped down inside his patrol car, barely alive. Bianca wasted no time but got his partner to the Johns Hopkins Hospital only a short distance away. The fatal bullet, fired by Toler, left doctors helpless. The wounded officer died minutes after his arrival in the emergency room.

Officers who arrived on the scene found Thomas Toler unconscious and barely alive with a bullet wound to the chest on McDonough Street. The detectives charged with finding the truth behind the incident could only guess at the final moments of both men, and surmised that Knight had confronted Toler as he ran from the alley near the intersection. The men had exchanged gunfire, with both suffering fatal chest wounds. Toler had collapsed where he was shot while Knight had made his way back to the patrol car to call for help over the radio. Officer Knight had lost consciousness with the radio in his hand, lacking even the strength to call for his fellow officers. Why Toler would do such a thing would never be known, which makes the loss of Officer Knight's life even more painful.

Patrolman John B. Bealefeld

September 10, 1945, Southern District
16 years and 6 months of service

Baltimore, a city rich in tradition and character, is also home to some of the most beautiful and interesting architecture on the East Coast. Most notable are the marble steps, usually five or six, that lead to the front doors of many rowhouses. Residents are diligent in their cleaning and care. Often, homeowners regard cleaning their steps as a way of putting forth their best appearance. But these attractive blocks of marble would prove fatal for forty-four-year-old Patrolman John Bealefeld.

On August 30, 1945, Patrolman Bealefeld went to 1526 Boyle Street in the Southern District to investigate a disturbance. When he arrived he met two brothers who were more than just an annoyance. From inside their house, Thomas and Joseph Geisler cursed and yelled in a menacing way, frightening neighbors and passersby. Bealefeld arrested them and led the way as they made their way through the front door. Neither brother was handcuffed as the pair walked out into the evening air. Joseph attempted to escape by crashing his fist onto the back of the officer's neck with all his strength.

As Bealefeld fell from the steps, he twisted awkwardly. His body hit the concrete sidewalk with so much force that the femur in his leg cracked in half. In intense pain, he shouted for help. Officers on the scene quickly subdued Geisler and called for medical care. John was transported to South Baltimore General Hospital. Several days passed and the commanders of the Southeastern District held Joseph Geisler on a large bail. On September 10, 1945, Lillian Bealefeld learned that her husband had died from an embolism resulting from his fractured leg, and that a Geisler had been charged with murder.

Patrolman Elmer A. Noon

November 20, 1946, Northeastern District
15 years and 5 months of service

Elizabeth Anne was only four years old by the time her father reached his fifteenth year serving the citizens of Baltimore. She looked forward to seeing him at the end of his workday, but sadly, late on a November afternoon, forty-one-year-old Elmer Noon would come home for the last time.

When Patrolman Noon arrived home just before six in the evening, his wife Elizabeth knew that something was very wrong and called for medical attention after putting her visibly ill husband in bed. By the time Dr. I. Earl Pass arrived, Elmer had died. The doctor determined that the cause of death was a massive heart attack.

His commanders and wife were confused by the cause of death because he had appeared to be in good shape and had not exhibited any of the warning signs and physical symptoms related to heart attack. Dr. Pass mentioned the possibility that great physical exertion by a healthy man sometimes results in a heart attack similar to the one Elmer Noon suffered. Investigators focused their attention on the his last call for service. At ten minutes before four o'clock, Noon and his partner, Patrolman Otte Leyhe, in Radio Car No. 23, had gone to the intersection of Gay and Forrest Streets, outside of the Bel Air Market, to help a Special Police Officer who was attempting to subdue a man who was large, strong, and drunk. Citizens were watching as the much larger Albert Thomas tossed Officer Fred Thomas from side to side.

Before their patrol car had come to a full stop, Noon had leapt from his passenger seat and joined the fight. Leyhe had not made it to the tussling officers before he saw Rogers toss Noon aside. Elmer was thrown with so much force that his feet did not touch the ground until he slammed into the side of the police vehicle. Stunned but not knocked out of the fight, Elmer fought to get a device known as the "iron claw," the precursor to the modern day handcuff, on Rogers' wrist. After what Officer Leyhe estimated was a five-to-ten minute fight, another officer, Patrolman William Ervin, arrived and helped subdue Rogers. It took four officers to control the violent man until the patrol wagon, driven by Patrolman Hugh Law, came to take him to the Northeast District. Once the wagon arrived the fight resumed. Rogers resisted just as violently when the officers tried to load him into the transport vehicle.

Elmer Noon had to ride with the wagon man to the station to keep Rogers from escaping or assaulting anyone else. The struggle continued all during the ride and into the holding cell. Despite repeated assaults by the drunken Rogers, Noon declined to charge him with the crime, lodging against him only the offense of disorderly conduct. After a commute of more than an hour, he arrived home, greeted his wife and child, and went to lie down. At six o'clock in the evening, Elmer was dead.

Members of his family waited anxiously for the outcome of the investigation into his death. Without the determination that it had occurred in the line of duty and the modest financial benefit that decision would permit, Elizabeth faced a difficult time raising their daughter on her own. Fortunately, such would not turn out to be the case. On January 7, 1947, Raymond Noon wrote a letter to the commissioner praising the department's decision to consider his brother's death in the line of duty, saying that "the decision rendered is a credit to the Department and proves that the men in charge have the interest of those under them at heart."

Patrolman Fred R. Unger

January 13, 1947, Central District
2 years and 8 months of service

After holding up a cabdriver on Saratoga Street near Gay, a gunman strolled through the Central District looking for another victim to rob. Armed with a .25 caliber semi-automatic pistol, the robber found his next target in the 900 block of Brevard Street. A description of the suspect was given to patrol officers who canvassed the area aggressively. Officer Fred Unger and his partner, Officer George Pfaff, cruised down Cathedral, keeping a sharp eye for signs of the thief. What they saw was a man running down the street. Unbeknownst to them was the fact that he had just attempted a second hold-up.

Unger and Pfaff caught up to the suspect at the intersection of Park and Preston Streets. With his window rolled down, Officer Unger called, "What are you running for?" The man strolled up to the car, pulled his gun from his waistband and coldly fired into Unger's head and body. Officer Pfaff was not struck and got out of the car to obtain a position of advantage. The suspect then fled on foot toward Howard Street. Pfaff ran hard after him but lost the suspect in the area of Dolphin Street and Linden Avenue. When Officer Pfaff returned to the patrol car, he found his friend had been shot in the face.

Pfaff put out a description of the gunman over the radio, and Officers Joseph Levin and John T. Griffin were quick to pick up the trail. At the corner of Morris Alley and Dolphin Street, they met with the same weapon that had fatally wounded Patrolmen Unger. Levin and Griffin were ready. When the suspect turned and fired, they felled him quickly in a blast of gunfire. Afterward, Levin and Griffin approached the lifeless body of Officer Unger's murderer. Among the things found on the gunman's body was money from the cab hold-up and his identity, Milfred E. Davis.

Patrolman Joseph D. Benedict

February 13, 1948, Northern District
6 years, 3 months of service

The cabdriver sat in his darkened cab, thinking that he was about to lose his life to the criminal who was holding him at gunpoint, and desperately hoping that someone would see him and send for help. Unfortunately, it was four o'clock on a Friday morning, and the chance that a passerby would notice the holdup was slim. Then he breathed a sigh of relief. An officer had seen his darkened but occupied cab parked on 33rd Street near the Alameda and was making his way over to investigate.

Roy Arnold Wood held his pistol tight and aimed deliberately, his eyes fixed on the approaching policeman. Officer Joseph Benedict was helpless against the spray of bullets from the suspect's gun, but his mere presence saved the cab driver's life. Wood fled to his home, where he told his girlfriend, Mary Bates Tolliver, what he had done. While officers combed the city for a suspect described as "twenty-four to twenty-eight years old, 160 to 170 pounds, sandy hair, wearing a full-length tan coat and a multicolored scarf around his neck," Roy Wood hid. For days afterward, the description was rebroadcast to keep the image fresh in every officer's mind.

A newspaper salesman, Regis King, who worked a newsstand at the corner of Greenmount and North Avenues, walked to a two-man patrol car parked at the corner and handed them a paper with the latest story about the slain officer. As he handed the paper through the open window, the description was broadcast once more. The radio message stuck with King throughout the day as he handed out newspapers, reminding him of the fallen officer, until an image began to come clear. The description was that of a man he knew as "Woody," who lived on 23rd Street. King called the Northern District and told Sergeant Maxwell that the description fit Mr. Wood "to a T." Officers were sent to Roy Wood's house on 23rd Street, where the landlord let them in. Ms. Tolliver was there. Fortunately for Officer Benedict's family and the department, she had a conscience and turned in Wood.

Sentenced to hang for the murder of Officer Benedict, Wood took his own life in his cell. On March 22, 1948, prison guards found him lifeless with his tie tightly wrapped around his neck. Officer Benedict left a wife and five children.

Patrolman Thomas J. Burns

October 1, 1948, Traffic Division – Motors Unit, 10 months of service

Officers in the Motors Unit are a special breed. Their pride and professionalism are manifest in the care and treatment of their motorcycles. They are often called upon for ceremonial and other important events as a way for the Baltimore Police Department to put its best foot forward. And too often they are called to duty to provide escort services for officers killed in the line of duty. It is this close association with funerals and memorial ceremonies that makes it especially hard for the members of the department to come to terms with the death of one of their own.

Officer Thomas Burns was no exception to the rule of pride and professionalism within the Motors Unit. His motorcycle gleamed as he rode down Erdman Avenue near the intersection of North Point Road when, without warning, a truck driver made a left turn directly into his path. With no time to react, Officer Burns crashed into the side of the truck. The truck driver's simple traffic violation of failing to yield the right-of-way cost Officer Burns his life.

The twenty-three-year-old officer had served with the U.S. Army during World War II, and had also served as a Park Policeman. At the time of his death he was unmarried and lived at home with his parents.

Patrolman John W. Arnold

December 30, 1948, Northwestern District
28 years and 2 months of service

On December 12, 1948, at about 6:30 A.M., a woman was in desperate need of help in the 900 block of Little Pine Street. Her enraged boyfriend had pinned her against a fence, wrapped his hands around her neck, and was squeezing the life out of her. Officers John Arnold and Norman Mike answered the call to "investigate the trouble" at the intersection of Argyle Avenue and Biddle Street. When they arrived, a citizen standing at the intersection pointed them toward the scene of the attack.

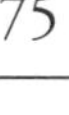

As they drove down the alley, they saw the woman being attacked by one Edward Grear. The officers left their car and rushed to her aid. Their arrival stopped the attack and saved the woman's life, but she she was unable to speak, or to warn the policemen that Grear was armed with a .45 caliber semi-automatic pistol. Grear spun around and fired five shots. Officers Arnold and Mike fell to the ground, both stricken several times.

Officer Mike would recover from his wounds, but his partner would lie in agony at Maryland General Hospital for eighteen days before succumbing to his injuries on December 30, 1948. He was an inspiration to his fellow officers and earned the nickname "Happy." At the time of his death, he was fifty-three years old.

Patrolman James L. Joyce

April 4, 1949, Northern District
8 years and 10 months of service

Late in the evening on April 3, 1949, Officer James Joyce cruised near the city line on Falls Road. Just past West Lake Avenue, Joyce steered his patrol car among the brick, Cape Cod–style houses and watched people walking along Falls. He delighted in talking with the residents of the neighborhoods and stopped close to the bridge that spanned the Pennsylvania Railroad to have a word with William Brookhart and his brother Benjamin. The bridge looks out over the Jones Falls Valley, and the trees would have just been coming to life after a long winter. The forty-two-year-old patrolman was behind the wheel of his patrol car, as he sat in this peaceful place.

Frank Love drove his car down Falls Road toward the three men as they conversed. Frank's good friend Richard Farace was with him as he traveled southbound across the bridge. Both were Loyola College students and well-known for their athletic abilities. Richard, a U.S. Navy veteran was celebrating his recent success in signing a contract with the Pittsburgh Pirates. For reasons that will never be known, Frank lost control of his car and struck a guardrail as he crossed the bridge. All Patrolman Joyce and the Brookhart brothers could do was watch as two tons of steel careened toward them.

The front of Frank Love's car crushed the driver's side door of the police car and smashed it into the guardrail. Love's car was demolished; Richard was killed instantly. The collision was nearly head-on and the two cars came to rest facing north on the east side of the street. Joyce was pinned behind the wheel of his patrol car and felt the pain from a broken pelvis, ribs, and punctured lungs. Help came quickly and the injured men were transported to Union Memorial Hospital. After several transfusions of blood and hours of treatment, Patrolman James Joyce succumbed to his injuries on April 4, 1949.

The community did its best to deal with the loss of two highly respected men. For days afterward, the patrolman and the ball player's pictures were seen side by side in the city's newspapers. No charges were filed against Frank Love, as investigators ruled the collision a freak accident. Goldie R. Joyce was left with her grief as she buried her husband in the Holy Redeemer Cemetery on April 8, 1949.

Patrolman Thomas J. O'Neill

October 16, 1949, Traffic Division – Motors Unit, 10 years and 4 months of service

The call came into the Motors Unit for an emergency escort for a polio patient to go from his home near the intersection of Liberty Heights and Rodgers Avenues, to Sydenham Hospital around 10 P.M. on October 15, 1949. As he had done many times before, Thomas O'Neill, along with two of his side partners, Officers Patrick Newman and Robert Kemmerzell, started their motorcycles, preparing to provide the escort that would weave through the busiest streets of the city. When a motorcycle unit has to perform an escort, it puts its own physical safety in danger every minute. In order to get a high priority vehicle like an ambulance smoothly through congested streets, motormen leapfrog one another from intersection to intersection, holding traffic at each. O'Neill and his partners worked methodically, accelerating past traffic, weaving through slower moving cars, and making sure the ambulance moved unimpeded.

When the escort reached the intersection of Greenmount Avenue and East 33rd Street, Officer O'Neill stopped his motorcycle to hold traffic. When he stepped off his bike, the engine stalled. He was able to hold the traffic but could not rejoin the escort. For several minutes he tried to restart his bike. Kick-starting a motorcycle is no easy task. It requires physical exertion, and in conjunction with the stresses of the police escort, O'Neill began to feel the effects of his effort.

Several minutes after the escort arrived at Sydenham Hospital, O'Neill rejoined Newman and Kemmerzell. He told them about the trouble he had had restarting his motorcycle and they then all made their way back to their posts. Newman and Kemmerzell rode off watching O'Neill as he turned toward Lake Montebello. Several minutes later, Dr. Richard Ferguson found O'Neill lying on the ground in need of help. Ferguson moved him into the Sydenham's emergency room, where physicians determined that his medical needs exceeded Sydenham's resources. An escort was arranged for him, and an ambulance took him from Sydenham to Mercy Hospital.

A combination of factors, including the stress of the escort and the effort of restarting his motorcycle, had induced a cerebral hemorrhage. Doctors worked for hours to save the policeman's life, but at 6:45 A.M. on October 16, 1949, Officer O'Neill died. After an investigation, Thomas O'Neill's widow, Helena, received a letter from George Brennan, Police Commissioner Ober's secretary, offering their sincerest condolences and confirming that Thomas' death was in the line of duty. Thomas O'Neill's personnel jacket was filled with letters from citizens expressing their appreciation for everything he had done on a daily basis, above and beyond the normal call of duty.

Patrolman Charles M. Hilbert

August 4, 1950, Headquarters
(Detailed to Traffic Control)
2 months of service

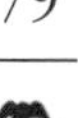

Sunday, August 4, 1950, was a day filled with automobile accidents, which claimed the lives of two and injured seven. Officer Charles Hilbert, recently married to Claire and new to the force, was assigned to operate the traffic control signal at the intersection of Potee Street and Patapsco Avenue. Traffic control is a perilous duty for several reasons. Motorists, busily navigating a congested roadway and planning what they are going to do at their destinations, are often out of touch with the pedestrians who pepper the sidewalks and crossing points. In addition to the dangers posed by passing automobiles, officers are sometimes tired or lulled to bored distraction by the simple, repetitive, mundane nature of controlling the flow of traffic. Before the use of electronic traffic lights, an officer had to change signs from "Stop" to "Go," and spent the better part of the day in the direct line of traffic.

Officer Hilbert had not been in the department long and still found all aspects of police work exciting. Unfortunately, he would not have the opportunity to spend much time in the service of the citizens of Baltimore. Either confused about finding his way through the notoriously dangerous intersection, or simply not paying attention to the officer in the path of his vehicle, Frank Constantine of Cockeysville, Maryland, struck Officer Hilbert, sending him flying through the air and into a pole and causing fatal internal injuries.

Constantine then lost complete control of his car and crashed into another fixed pole. Both men were sent to the South Baltimore General Hospital and treated. Constantine would recover from his fractured ribs and internal injuries. Officer Hilbert would die a few rooms away.

Twenty-seven-year-old Charles Hilbert was laid to rest one week later in his hometown of Wilkes-Barre, Pennsylvania.

PATROLMAN ROLAND W. MORGAN

January 6, 1951, Northern District
6 years and 4 months of service

William Conrad was idly watching the scenery pass by while riding his bus home when he saw what appeared to be a man lying in the street at the intersection of Roland Avenue and Upland Road. His shock turned to disbelief when he realized the body was that of a policeman in need of help. William leapt off the bus and sprinted to the side of the fallen officer. His heart sank—he was looking into the face of a man who had been his student in Sunday school. With no time to lose, he went to the patrol car and tried to use the radio to call for help. The driver's side door had been torn apart, with green paint smeared along the crushed side.

At approximately 11 P.M., with just over an hour left in his shift, Officer Roland Morgan had gone to a nearby call box to make his hourly call, a tool used by the department to account for officers throughout their tour of duty. It was cold on this January night as he walked around his car toward the call box. A car driven by John Caskie

Jr., who was drunk, careened out of control around the corner. Before he could get out of the way, Officer Morgan was crushed. Caskie's careless, indefensible decision to get behind the wheel cost this officer his life.

Making matters worse was the fact that Caskie did not stop. Fortunately, witnesses were able to provide information about the vehicle to aid in the identification of Mr. Caskie. While his fellow officers searched for their suspect, Officer Morgan died on the operating table at Union Memorial Hospital. Through the coordinated efforts of the state, county, and Baltimore City Police, Caskie was soon located, his car parked at the Valley Inn Tavern on Falls Road. He was charged with driving under the influence and failure to stop after an accident. When an officer loses his or her life in the line of duty, it is always a hard blow, but when an officer's life is taken because of a thoughtless, careless act like drunk driving, it is that much harder to accept.

Officer Morgan was loved by his community. He had grown up in the Northern District and was a welcome sight to his friends and neighbors when they needed help. Several businesses took up a collection to help his widow and children. The collection jars were adorned with his picture and the simple sentence, "You knew Officer Morgan." John Caskie killed not only a Baltimore City Police Officer, he killed Ruth's husband and Dorothy, Alice, and Audrey's father.

SERGEANT JAMES L. SCHOLL

August 1, 1953, Eastern District
11 years and 7 months of service

Early on the morning of July 20, 1953, a resident looking out his window near an East Baltimore tavern, Brown's Bar in the 1800 block of Broening Highway, saw a suspicious car. Fearing that someone might be planning to break into the closed business, he called police. When they arrived, they discovered that the car was indeed stolen. They felt the hood of the car to see if it was still warm. It was, indicating that the thieves were still nearby.

At approximately 3:20 A.M., Sergeant Scholl and a backup officer parked a safe distance away and began to walk toward the bar. The suspicions of the resident were correct. Sergeant Scholl and his partners, Officers Thomas Alford, Cecil Patterson, Benjamin Schwartz, and others, began to check the doors and windows of the business, moving along as quietly as they could. After a few moments, Officer Schwartz discovered an open window. More officers arrived until twelve were on hand, prepared to enter the business. Sergeant Scholl, as he often did, took the lead and crawled through the window, surprising a pair of burglars. Beauford Saunders and his friend Rodger Wyley, former army buddies who had both been dishonorably discharged, drew their pistols. A sharp gun battle broke out that left two men mortally wounded.

Sergeant Scholl was transported to City Hospital for treatment. Sanders died, and Wyley was apprehended at the scene. Sergeant Scholl held on for months, and all hoped that he would recover. Despite the best efforts of the best medical staff that the city had to offer, and more than two hundred donors of blood for the wounded sergeant, James Scholl died of his wounds on August 1, 1953. Eventually, Rodger Wyley would be charged with many crimes including the murder of Sergeant Scholl and burglary. For his bravery and valor, Sergeant Scholl was awarded the Medal of Honor by Commissioner Beverly Ober, posthumously.

Patrolman Alfred P. Bobelis

February 14, 1954, Southern District
11 years of service

The two cars collided with such force that they came to rest on the sidewalk at the intersection of Hanover and Randall Streets. The sound of the collision reverberated loudly through the neighborhood, and Officers Alfred Bobelis and Marvin March were immediately dispatched to help. They responded swiftly, and on their arrival saw that one of the drivers involved in the accident was running away. Calvin Luckey, from Philadelphia, fled because he did not have a license. The officers quickly decided that Bobelis would remain at the scene to safeguard the other crash victim and citizens gathering about the scene from oncoming traffic while Officer March gave chase. It was nearly three in the morning on February 14, and the frigid air bit into anyone who dared to be out on the streets. Cold and barely visible to oncoming traffic, Officer Bobelis did his best to warn approaching drivers to steer around the accident.

For whatever reason, Earle Kirkley of the 3400 block of Greenmount Avenue was driving recklessly and traveling well above the posted speed limit toward the intersection and Officer Bobelis. Kirkley hit Bobelis hard enough to propel him through the air. When his body slammed onto the street, his skull and both legs were fractured. Only minutes before, Officer March had succeeded in arresting Calvin Luckey and was on his way back to the accident scene, but Officer Bobelis's injuries were mortal. Officer March could not have saved him. Nevertheless, he took his fatally injured partner to the South Baltimore General Hospital, where he was pronounced dead upon arrival.

Kirkley would be convicted of manslaughter and numerous traffic violations, but no amount of jail time would ease the sense of loss shared by fellow officers and by Emma Bobelis and their daughters, twenty-one-year-old Constance and six-year-old Emily.

Patrolman Aubrey L. Lowman

April 19, 1954, Northwestern District
11 years and 5 months of service

On April 18, 1954, a car sat empty at the corner of Division and Mosher Streets. It had been stolen, but rather than approach it on his own, the owner, Carl Hickman, decided to call the police of the Northwestern District to recover it and hopefully apprehend the person responsible. Officer Aubrey Lowman, who had just relieved Officers Jasper and Kisler, stood in the shadows, looking for signs of the car thief and hoping to make an arrest. Shortly before midnight, a man and woman walked to the car and got inside. Officer Lowman had no way of knowing that the man in the car had recently been released from the state penitentiary after serving time for auto theft. Melvin Oliver knew that if caught, he would have no hope of a short sentence, yet despite this risk he continued to steal.

Officer Lowman approached the car cautiously but was taken by surprise when Oliver leaped out and began firing. His first shot struck Officer Lowman in his left shoulder as he attempted to draw his revolver to return fire. The second ripped into the abdomen as the officer fell to his knees. Officers Jasper and Kisler heard the shots and rushed back to help. They found Officer Lowman on his knees leaning against the stolen car and saw Oliver running from the scene. Unable to chase down Oliver, they focused their efforts on trying to save their friend's life, but at five minutes after midnight on April 19, 1954, Officer Lowman was pronounced dead.

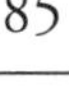

Citizens of the Northwestern neighborhoods organized search parties in an effort to locate Oliver, and off-duty officers reported to the station house as volunteers. Tension was high while all men remotely matching the killer's description were stopped and taken in for questioning. Oliver did what he could to hide and alter his appearance. He used his weapon to steal a change of clothes and remained ever vigilant. Yet Officers Howard Bayne and Gordon Holle of the Northeastern District were not fooled by Oliver's attempts to disguise. They spotted him as he walked down Gay Street. Realizing that he had been spotted, Oliver fired at the officers and ran away. He was soon out of sight and sought refuge in a parked car in the 1600 block of Eager Street.

A fourteen-year-old boy, seeing the officers searching for Oliver, flagged them down and pointed to the car in which Oliver was hiding. The boy, Howard Somerville, reported that he had seen the gunman take his own life. Appropriately cautious, Bayne and Holle approached the car with drawn pistols. The scene they encountered was grisly. Oliver's body was slumped over, and blood coated what appeared to be every surface of the car's interior. In the dead man's coat pocket was a simple note that revealed his absolute determination not to return to jail: "I taken a life. I give my life. I kill no more. . . ."

Officer Lowman left his wife, Dorothea, behind.

Patrolman Walter D. Davis

July 1, 1954, Northeastern District
1 year and 9 months of service

The police car's hood was folded nearly in half. The large concrete pillar it had crashed into was unscathed. In the early morning hours of July 1, 1954, Officer Walter Davis had been driving his patrol car down the 4400 block of Harford Road. Ten minutes earlier, other officers had radioed that the lighting along Harford Road had gone out and that it was difficult to see the safety pylons along the road. They had been erected to protect other structures from damage but now created a whole other problem. Several collisions resulting in death and serious injury had been attributed to the improper placement and lighting of these safety pylons, and nearly one year prior to Officer Davis' crash, city traffic director Henry Barnes had ordered that all pylons at the 143 intersections receive better lighting along with reflective sheeting.

The specific nature of the early morning crash, as well as any contributing factors, may never be known, but Officer Davis's patrol car smashed into an unlighted pylon at the intersection of Harford Road and Montebello Terrace. Investigators found more questions than answers. A review of the call history showed that Davis was not responding to a call for service, nor had he radioed an attempt to stop any vehicle traveling in the area. Walter Davis was found dead in his patrol car by officers responding to the scene of a crash called in by passersby. Smoke poured from the car as people worked to free Davis's body.

The thirty-year-old Patrolman was a veteran of the U.S. Army, was married to Doris, and was the proud father of two daughters. As a result of this loss and others like it, the remaining pylons throughout the city were removed.

Sergeant James J. Purcell

October 24, 1955, Northwestern District
16 years and 5 months of service

Sergeant James Purcell had worked as the supervisor for the Central District holding cells for many years. With five commendations, his service record was considered exemplary. He did his best to treat both his subordinates and inmates with respect and dignity. Such was the case on September 15, when federal agents booked a prisoner in the Central District Stationhouse for overnight holding. Arrested for tax evasion and other such crimes, Henry Grunewald was to be held overnight and looked after by Sergeant Purcell. Grunewald appreciated the special effort that the sergeant showed and expressed his thanks in the form of a cash gift of seventy-five dollars. Departments have strict rules against members accepting any type of gratuity and if it should happen, they are required to submit the gift and notify their chain of command.

Sergeant Purcell did not submit the gift but divided it among his subordinates. Word of his action reached some of the higher-ranking members of the department and an investigation found Purcell guilty of violating departmental procedure. The required penalty was termination. Rather than end the career of a man who had spent so many years in faithful, commendable service, Commissioner James Hepbron, newly appointed to his position after years of service on the Baltimore City Parole Board, decided to show leniency, and merely demoted him. Agreeable to the terms of his punishment, now Patrolman Purcell chose to support his family and was thankful for not being unemployed.

As one of his last official acts as a parole board member, Commissioner Hepbron had also agreed to parole Ronald King, a criminal with an extensive record for crimes such as armed robbery. Set in motion by the steps taken by one man, a fatal meeting between King and Purcell would eventually take place in a dark hallway, with tragic consequences for both.

In the early morning hours of October 23, 1955, Patrolman Purcell was working in a radio car with his partner Patrolman Charles Ernest, who would lose his life in the line of duty almost ten years later. They received a call from a frantic woman who occupied the first floor apartment across the street from 134 West Lanvale Street and who told police she had seen a man climb through the first floor window of a three-story house. Purcell and Ernest made their way to the house along with Patrolmen Richard Doda, John Boyle, Leroy Prediger, and William Bromwell. While Doda and Boyle secured the outside of the house to prevent the burglar's escape, Purcell and Ernest entered the dwelling and began a methodical search. Crouched behind a large piece of furniture in the second floor hallway was the recently paroled Ronald King.

Purcell searched the second floor apartment of Miss Florence Kelly and entered the dark hallway. His flashlight beam fell on King's hiding place, and he called out to the burglar, "Come out . . . you have no business here!" Purcell's partner, alerted by the shouting, ran to his partner's side. King leapt from his hiding place and ripped Purcell's weapon from its holster. A brief, violent struggle ensued but ended as quickly as it began. Before Ernest could help, King struck Purcell in the face with the butt of the pistol and fired a single shot into his abdomen. James Purcell fell to his knees and quietly said, "I'm shot . . . get an ambulance . . . I'm dying." King bolted down the narrow staircase and was met by Patrolman Prediger who was rushing upstairs toward the sound of gunfire. King got past Prediger, who fired a shot, and then attempted to escape by breaking the frosted windowpane of the front door with the pistol. Prediger leveled his revolver and fired five times into King. Despite his wounds, King opened the door and fired two shots at Patrolman Doda, who shot back, hitting King twice more. King stumbled through the doorway and collapsed at the bottom of the front steps, dead.

Purcell was taken to Maryland General Hospital, where he died twenty-three hours later. James Purcell left a widow and three sons behind. Shortly afterward, many people contemplated the life of a man who was known for his jovial disposition. Commissioner Hepbron along with Governor Theodore McKeldin sought to restore the deceased patrolman's rank to sergeant to help his family with the expenses they now faced. The governor announced that he was "confident that through his bravery, his ability and his general integrity in the line of duty he would have won back his sergeancy had he lived." Eventually, with the support of the governor and commissioner, the city council restored Purcell's rank to sergeant posthumously.

Patrolman John R. Phelan

September 29, 1956, Northwestern District
4 months of service

A special picture of John Phelan hangs in his nephew's office. The photograph of a rookie who dreamed of nothing but police work as a career, is balanced by the unique patch of the Baltimore Police Department within its custom frame. To look at this picture of a young man, full of life and with unquestioned pride in his eyes, makes one contemplate his own mortality. At the age of twenty-one and with only four months of service protecting the City of Baltimore, John died in the back of an ambulance, the victim of a bullet from his own pistol. His nineteen-year-old widow, Jacqueline, described her late husband's love for police work as if it were a religion, and spoke of the many times he would arrange his uniform until he felt it was perfect and clean the revolver he had worked so hard to earn. Sadly, the young man was killed before the birth of his first child.

The neighborhoods in the Northwest District lived in fear, as a gang of armed robbers ravaged businesses at will. Officer Phelan bravely patrolled the areas hardest hit by the robberies. In an effort to catch the robbers in the act, several officers hid in the back rooms of liquor stores and grocery stores and patiently waited for crime to strike. Patrolman Wilbert J. Elsroad Jr. hid in the rear of Parks' Liquor Store in the 2700 block of West North Avenue. Late on the evening of September 29, 1956, three men burst through the front door of the liquor store brandishing handguns. They began shouting orders to store owner William Parks and his two employees, Gilbert Donahue and James Cornish. On emerging from his hiding place, Patrolman Elsroad was met with gunfire from less than ten feet away. Bullets flew, shattering bottles and emptying cases of beer, but, amazingly, not a single person was struck, and the three robbers fled to the street with Elsroad close behind. Elsroad took aim at the largest member of the group and let his final round fly. It struck Alvin Herbert Braxton, a six-foot, 210-pound, seventeen-year-old in his leg as he ran. The shot stopped the huge juvenile in his tracks. Elsroad went to the nearest phone and called for assistance.

With news of the gun battle spreading fast, the request for assistance was quickly answered. Among those who responded were Patrolman Phelan and his partner, Patrolman Theodore Weintraub. With the scene secured, the officers sent for an ambulance to care for the young criminal's leg wound. Medics Walter Robinson and Mark Rohm arrived shortly afterward and loaded the critically injured man into their ambulance. In the mid-1950s, handcuffs and leg irons were luxury items. Often, those patrolmen who had them had spent their own money to acquire them. On this night not a single responding patrolman had a set of handcuffs to restrict the movements of the prisoner. In order to properly guard against escape, Phelan and Weintraub joined the medics in the back of the ambulance for the ride to Lutheran Hospital. Braxton saw an opportunity to escape and began to fight despite the throbbing pain in his leg. The two patrolmen fought back in a desperate struggle within the close quarters of the ambulance.

The medics stopped their vehicle in the intersection of Poplar Grove and Baker Streets and went to aid the patrolmen. Before Robinson and Rohm could help, Braxton ripped Phelan's gun from his holster and began firing wildly. He managed to shoot his way to temporary freedom by fatally wounding Phelan and hitting Weintraub in both legs. The violent youth forced open the doors to the ambulance and assaulted a taxi cab driver who had stopped nearby. He next took control of the car and rammed the rear of the ambulance to keep the patrolmen inside. By this time, others were responding to the sound of gunfire and frightened calls from citizens. Patrolman Henry Hau was first on the scene and shot Braxton four more times. With their damaged ambulance, Robinson and Rohm sped to the hospital in an attempt to save the two patrolmen's lives. John Phelan died before he reached the hospital, the youngest to lose his life in the service of the city. Eventually Patrolman Weintraub would recover from his wounds.

Patrolmen Philip Buratt and William DePaola, who were driving a patrol wagon, responded to the scene. Still without handcuffs, they transported the wounded Braxton to Lutheran Hospital for much needed care, but once at the hospital, Braxton again fought with all his strength despite his extensive wounds. This time he was subdued by an overwhelming number of police who finally handcuffed him. After he had received the necessary care, Braxton revealed the names of his fellow gang members and where they could be found. Police arrested and charged Alvin Braxton, Roger Ray, Earl Pickett, and Albert Braxton, Alvin's older brother, with more than eleven robberies. The gang had stolen nearly $36,000 dollars and three pistols. Alvin Braxton was also tried and convicted of John Phelan's murder.

If anything good could come from such a tragic moment, it was the public outcry over the fact that officers were not properly equipped. Newspaper editorials insisted on properly funding and equipping the Baltimore Police Department. One editorial looked upon the idea as a matter of common sense. "Certainly relatively small budget items should not stand in the way of maximum protective equipment for all policemen." The editor went on to suggest that "Taxpayers would be far from hostile to inclusion of relatively small sums for general issuance of both handcuffs and new holsters."

These measures did little to assuage young Jacqueline's grief at the loss of her husband, but they did promise that in the future officers would have the added measure of safety that many now take for granted.

Patrolman John F. Andrews

October 9, 1957, Traffic Division – Motors Unit, 2 years of service

The grim task of investigating the fatal crash fell into the hands of the city's most talented detectives. In a crime scene several hundred feet long, a number of police officers and detectives noted every detail and tried to piece together the last events of Patrolman John Andrews' life. Because he had been unable to radio into headquarters what he was attempting to do, many questions remained. The absolute truth of Patrolman Andrews' death may never be known.

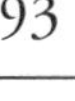

Possibly Patrolman Andrews was attempting to overtake a speeder traveling approximately seventy-five miles per hour. In the 900 block of South Monroe Street Andrews's Harley Davidson motorcycle roared, emergency lights flashed, and the siren wailed. The speeding motorist drifted into the path of the patrolman's bike, forcing Andrews to swerve to avoid a collision. Andrews lost control of the bike. There was no chance of recovery as man and machine slammed into a wall and began to tumble sideways. Patrolman Andrews was entangled in the wreckage as it flipped. His body was thrown clear and came to rest over a hundred feet farther on from where the motorcycle came to rest.

Patrolman Andrews suffered a massive skull fracture as he tumbled and was pronounced dead when he arrived at St. Agnes Hospital.

The driver of the speeding vehicle was never identified. The thirty-four-year-old patrolman had spent several years in the service of his country and away from his family during World War II. He had survived three years of fierce combat in the Pacific, but it turned out to be the dangers of home that left his wife Agnes a widow.

Patrolman Robert K. Nelson

September 19, 1958, Traffic Division – Motors Unit, 1 year and 6 months of service

Robert Nelson had but recently joined the Baltimore Police Department when he heard the news of the death of motorcycle Patrolman John Andrews as the result of the reckless actions of a speeding motorist. Twenty days before the anniversary of Andrews' death, Robert Nelson would lose his life to the careless and criminal actions of a motorist as well. Like many of his fellow officers, Nelson had served his country in the armed forces before serving his community as a patrolman. From 1950 to 1953, the height of the Korean Conflict, he bravely served in the U.S. Army. Patrolman Nelson maintained his military bearing when it came to policing.

On Tuesday September 16, 1958, Nelson piloted his motorcycle into the intersection of Gay Street and Broadway. As he entered the intersection an automobile driven by Richard F. Bishop from Trenton, New Jersey, struck him. Bishop's careless and negligent actions had the effect of hurling Nelson flying more than twenty feet through the air. He landed head first against a curb, fracturing his skull and knocking him unconscious. Moments later, doctors at St. Joseph's

Hospital were working to save his life. Nelson's commander assigned an officer to bring his wife Emma to the hospital from her home at 1652 William Avenue.

When she arrived the doctors were using all the tools and techniques they had to save Robert's life. They performed extensive and invasive brain surgery and inserted a silver plate to treat the massive fracture, but the injury had resulted in too much damage. Robert never regained consciousness and died three days later, on September 19, 1958, with Emma by his side. Richard Bishop had only been in town for two days and would now be held on charges of automobile manslaughter.

Patrolman Richard H. Duvall, Jr.

January 11, 1959, Northwestern District
6 years and 3 months of service

Since its creation in the mid-nineteenth century, Druid Hill Park has been one of the city's jewels. It is home to the city's famous zoo as well as miles of walking paths through lush, green, beautiful woods. In addition to an expansive, serene lake are excellently crafted, architecturally impressive structures. For years, citizens have sought the refuge of this peaceful place, but where law-abiding citizens find tranquil spaces, criminals often find many places to hide.

It was the middle of winter when Officer Richard Duvall's siren wailed as he chased a stolen car down the 3800 block of Greenspring Avenue. The leaves had long since fallen and the park offered a different type of refuge for criminals. The car thief knew that if he made it to the park, he had a good chance of escaping in the setting sun, but with the park in sight, he lost control of the car and rammed an embankment. He bailed out and began to run.

Officer Duvall and his back-up officers caught up with him in a nearby alley and the fight began. Several officers jumped on top of the suspect and worked to control him. One had his service revolver in his hand and did not holster his weapon before he joined the struggle. Suddenly it accidentally discharged. The bullet found Officer Duvall's heart as he fought with the car thief, killing Duvall instantly. Only one other time in the history of the Baltimore City Police Department has an officer died from a fellow officer's bullet. Though no officer should lose his life in the performance of his or her duty, tragedy is hardest to accept when an officer is inadvertently killed by one of his own.

Officer Duvall's wife, Charlotte, and his two daughters Susan and Cheryl laid him to rest in Loudon Park Cemetery.

In loving memory of my father. Valerie Eckert Eigner

PATROLMAN WARREN V. ECKERT

November 16, 1960, Traffic Division – Motors Unit, 5 years and 1 month of service

Thirty-eight years to the day after Officer Warren Eckert died in the line of duty, his daughter Valerie stood beside his grave once more. She had been only nine years old on the day her father died. In the early afternoon, with his lights and sirens on, he was attempting to catch a speeder when he collided with a large beverage truck in the intersection of Pratt and Carey Streets. The truck driver had done his best to come to a stop, but the collision could not be avoided. Thrown from his motorcycle, Officer Eckert received massive head injuries. He had been taken to Franklin Square Hospital where doctors Van Wisse and Mossberg had pronounced him dead.

Warren Eckert had been a proud and professional officer during his five years of service. He had kept his motorcycle in pristine condition and his uniform sharp in every detail. Although he was dedicated to his profession, he had always held his family on a higher level. He sometimes brought his motorcycle home for his girls to see. As proud as he was of his service as a police officer and in the navy, he was prouder still of his daughters Valerie, Beverly, and Maureen, and his wife Katherine.

Valerie's work with the Make-A-Wish foundation, a group that helps terminally ill children fulfill seemingly impossible dreams, would take her back to the days of her own childhood and memories of her father. One especially poignant call to the foundation came in on August 7, 1998, from Joy Goldberger, a Child Life Specialist at Johns Hopkins Children's Center. She told Valerie the story of a young man named Brian whose goal in life was to become a police officer but who was losing his battle with Hepatitis C. Brian did not want to be any kind of police officer—he wanted "to be the kind of policeman that rides a motorcycle." Valerie was deeply moved. Since her husband had been a Baltimore Police Officer and her father had been a motorman, she quickly agreed to Mrs. Goldberger's request.

Brian's wish found enthusiastic support within the department and garnered substantial coverage in the local newspapers. Valerie wanted his wish to be more than just a swearing in ceremony and she found help in a man who would become a very good friend. Lt. Carl Gutberlet made it possible to bring a departmental motorcycle into the Johns Hopkins Hospital for Brian. Things were falling into place and Valerie believed that her father was watching over her. On Sep-

tember 23, a full uniform was assembled for Brian to wear when Commissioner Frazier swore him in. A late night call that same day to Lieutenant Gutberlet resulted in a last-minute police escort home for Brian when he was discharged from the hospital.

Thirty-eight years after Warren Eckert's death, nearly to the hour, a line of Harley-Davidson police motorcycles led Brian's funeral procession into Cedar Hill Cemetery. Valerie sat next to Lieutenant Gutberlet as the Honor Guard marched with precision, and thought of her father.

PATROLMAN HENRY SMITH, JR.

April 7, 1962, Central District
4 years and 8 months of service

Officer Henry Smith Jr. served his nation in the Korean War with the U.S. Marine Corps, facing death for three years from May 24, 1951, to May 23, 1954, in battles with North Korean and Chinese forces. Although he had done more for his nation than most, service was in his heart. When he returned from military duty, he joined the Baltimore Police Department. He was off-duty the night of April 7, 1962, when he came across a dice game outside a tavern in the 700 block of West Lexington Street.

He decided to identify himself as a police officer and break up the game. Gambling is one of many nuisance crimes that lead to the degradation of a neighborhood. To let the gamblers know that he would not tolerate this particular disregard for the law, he ordered them to stop what they were doing and leave the area. In response, the two men involved in the game attacked him. They wrestled him to the ground and began to pry his revolver from his holster. Two patrolmen in the area were drawn to the commotion and went to help their fellow officer. As they got closer, they saw one of the men standing over Officer Smith, firing his service revolver into his body. Patrolmen James Thompson and William Cromer of the Western District opened fire, wounding the assailant. Patrolman Chris Kessler found the wounded thirty-year-old suspect in the 100 block of North Pine Street.

Officer Smith died at the scene, and his weapon was found in the alleyway next to 702 West Fayette Street. Henry Smith was thirty-one years old at the time of his death and left a wife and five children.

Patrolman Richard D. Seebo

May 26, 1962, Traffic Division – Motors Unit
2 years and 10 months of service

Patrolman Richard Seebo leaned into the turn from Barclay Street onto westbound East 20th Street and brought his Harley-Davidson alongside a 1955 green and white Pontiac driven by Wallace Creighton. Seebo ordered Creighton to stop. Seebo was known for his strict enforcement of all the traffic codes and his serious attitude toward policing. The 300 block of East 20th Street is lined with traditional Baltimore rowhouses near the Greenmount Cemetery and is barely two blocks away from the very spot where Patrolman Frederick Kontner would lose his life in the line of duty five years later.

Creighton waited for the patrolman to park the motorcycle behind his car, then shifted into reverse and slammed into the unsuspecting officer. The crash was violent but Seebo managed to escape serious injury. He regained his feet and ordered Creighton from the car. He told his assailant that he was under arrest and called upon passersby to use their telephones to call in for assistance. Creighton saw an opportunity to escape. When no citizen could offer the necessary help for the officer, Wallace Creighton pushed away from Seebo and pulled out a .32 caliber handgun. Creighton fired point blank into the officer's chest. Seebo staggered to the sidewalk and collapsed, face down. The defenseless officer could do nothing to stop Creighton as he pulled his departmental revolver from its holster and fired a third shot into Seebo's back.

Shortly after the shooting, Henry Ben Huff, a passenger in Creighton's car, was arrested and grilled regarding the whereabouts of Seebo's killer. It was quickly determined that Creighton had plans to leave Maryland and head south. Creighton avoided capture when a National Park Policeman stopped him as he made his way to North Carolina. The description of Seebo's murderer had been distributed but had not made it to all departments quickly enough. In another routine traffic stop, Creighton decided against attacking the officer but readily offered that he was on his way to Heathspring, North Carolina.

The intense hunt for Creighton soon brought results. A coordinated East Coast effort located the murderer in South Carolina. He was brought back to Baltimore to face charges and helped to bring closure for Richard Seebo's wife, Patricia, and daughters Patricia and Phyllis. Less than a month and a half after Patrolman Henry Smith died, the Baltimore Police family felt the pain of loss again.

Patrolman Edward J. Kowalewski

July 2, 1962, Central District
8 years of service

Helen Kowalewski sobbed uncontrollably as she waited in the sterile hallway of Mercy Hospital. When she was able to fight back the tears, she recalled how the bad news had made its way to her. "I have a knocker that nobody uses but the police, the last time was when he had his heart attack," she said. Less than a year before, her husband had been in the same building recovering from that heart attack. Now Patrolman Edward Kowalewski again lay in a bed receiving the best available care as he clung to life, and his stricken wife sat in a chair barely fifty feet from his hospital room door.

Just after one o'clock in the morning of July 2, 1962, Patrolman Kowalewski was investigating a routine matter at the North Inn on North Avenue when he heard gunshots nearby. Raymond Rich, a District of Columbia cabdriver, had picked up a fare in Washington and headed for Baltimore. It was a long drive, and his passenger seemed anxious to find particular people as they checked several different addresses. Ray Allen Nixt, a forty-one-year-old parole violator recently released from the violent Folsom Prison in California, carried his nickel-plated .38 caliber pistol wherever he went. When Rich was ready to abandon what he thought was an inane search, he demanded the fare money so he could return home. Instead of payment, Rich received two bullets in the back.

Patrolman Kowalewski was sprinting toward the sound of those shots when he met Nixt on the street. Neither man spoke a word.

Kowalewski tried to draw his weapon when he saw the glint of reflected light from Nixt's pistol. The confrontation lasted only a moment, as Nixt fired two shots into Kowalewski's chest. Two cabdrivers, Charles and Zonnie Wise, witnessed this senseless act. Charles was waiting for a fare when Nixt jumped into the back of the cab and pressed the pistol's barrel against the cabby's head. Nixt barked orders to drive away quickly. He screamed into Charles' ear that he had "just shot two men down the street, so you better drive like hell." To preserve his own life, Charles took off, blowing his horn as he ran red lights.

Ernest Clements, a passenger in Zonnie Wise's cab and a veteran infantryman from World War II, pleaded with Zonnie to give chase. The men were enraged by the brazen shooting of a policeman and took off after the armed man. In the early morning hours the two cabs wound through the deserted streets. A third cab joined the chase as Nixt fired through the rear window of Charles' cab. When the speeding cars passed by the Bel Air Market, Zonnie pulled to the roadside and picked up Patrolman Stanley Zawadzki. Nixt fired his last shot near the intersection of North and Guilford Avenues. The chase continued until the two cabs pinned Charles' cab to a stop at Orleans and Gay Streets. As the men converged on Nixt, he attempted to reload his pistol. Charles Wise reached into the back seat and grabbed it, preventing Nixt from firing again. Ray Nixt held his hands above his head as Patrolman Zawadzki shouted at him to surrender. With no avenue of escape left, Nixt gave up. Police soon learned that Nixt was a holdup man that had terrorized his Washington, D.C., neighborhood and had come to Baltimore to continue his violent work.

Patrolman Zawadzki had captured the man who had caused Edward Kowalewski's fatal wounds. That would be the only good news Helen and her sons would hear that day. Doctors needed blood for transfusions to keep Edward alive, and the volunteers all wore the Baltimore City Police uniform. The family gathered outside Edward's

room and conversed in Polish so his father could understand everything that was occurring. Then a nurse gravely approached the tightly clustered family and pulled Helen aside to tell her she could see him and say her goodbye. She entered the room and spoke to her husband, the father of their four sons, Edward, Wayne, Joseph, and Charles. Shortly afterward, Dr. Harold Biehl announced that Edward had died at ten o'clock in the morning. The bullets had torn his liver and a main vein connected to his heart.

Patrolman Francis R. Stransky

January 10, 1964, Central District
5 years of service

Nineteen sixty-four was the most violent year in the history of the Baltimore Police Department. By year's end five officers would die in the line of duty: Patrolmen Francis Stransky, Claude Profili, Walter Matthys, Teddy Bafford, and Sergeant Jack Cooper. Officers Profili, Matthys, Bafford, and Sergeant Cooper would all be shot to death. From a seventeen-year veteran sergeant to a rookie with barely five days of duty on the street, each was a man of valor, whose loss was deeply felt.

The first to die was Francis R. Stransky, the thirty-nine-year-old husband of Eva and father of Francis Jr. and Virginia. A policeman in the Central District for five years, Francis enjoyed patrolling the area around Cicero's in the Bel Air Market. He liked the people in the area as well as the good places to catch a bite to eat.

Just before six in the evening, in the 500 block of Ensor Street,

Stransky arrested Larry G. Wadsworth, a twenty-two-year-old man, for a minor charge. Wadsworth decided to fight the patrolman and quickly found that he was overmatched. Not only did Stransky subdue him, he had to take Wadsworth to Mercy Hospital for treatment of the wounds he had inflicted with blows with his nightstick. After the visit was completed, the two men walked to the Central District Station so the prisoner could be booked. While Wadsworth was waiting in the holding cell, Stransky collapsed in the roll call room, and died from a massive heart attack. Less than an hour after leaving Mercy with his prisoner, Francis Stransky was pronounced dead. An autopsy was performed and Wadsworth was held pending the outcome. Doctors determined that the cause of the heart attack was the struggle with Wadsworth. In addition to a simple disturbance charge, Wadsworth was then charged with assault and causing the patrolman's death.

For the first time in well over a year, the members of the Baltimore Police Department mourned the loss of one of their own. Thus began a very deadly year in the department's history.

Patrolman Claude J. Profili

February 6, 1964, Western District
12 years and 1 month of service

On January 29, 1964, at 1:35 P.M., three men entered the National Bank's West Baltimore office at 520 Franklintown Road and began to execute their plans of armed robbery with seemingly perfect precision. While two of them worked to steal more than

$23,000 from the tellers, the third watched the door for police. They moved quickly in order to complete their heist before anyone could trigger the alarm. In that they failed. Despite their speed and the element of surprise, someone sounded the alarm and police were on their way. The three were still in the bank when veteran patrolman Claude Profili cautiously made his way to the entrance. Assistant Cashier Walter Haynie was standing near the front door and saw Profili as he opened it. Haynie was unable to warn him as he came inside.

Too late, Patrolman Profili saw the robbers and the fact that they were armed. As he began to retreat, one of them ordered, "Hold it, just keep coming in." Profili knew that his window of opportunity to escape with his life was fast closing, but he saw only two armed men and believed he could get out and summon assistance. He was drawing his pistol and backing out of the door when the third man fired, striking Patrolman Profili in the head. He stumbled out the front door and collapsed on the sidewalk. This violent turn hastily changed the criminals' plans, and they fled outside. They made their escape, and the manhunt began.

Patrolman Profili was on an operating table in Lutheran Hospital within ten minutes of the shooting. Doctors discovered that the bullet had broken into two parts when it entered. They were able to remove one fragment but not the other. Claude Profili would never regain consciousness or even know that his wife Clara and daughter Cynthia were by his side. On February 6, 1964, the thirty-five-year-old Baltimore native succumbed to his wounds. The FBI was quick to offer help with the massive manhunt. Hard detective work paid off with the arrest of Vincent Chebat Jr., the man who had fired the fatal shot.

Patrolman Walter P. Matthys

September 11, 1964, Eastern District
3 months of service

Fresh from the academy and newly married, Walter Matthys walked his post with the pride and enthusiasm that every good rookie has. The care and acclimation of a new police officer is not the sole responsibility of the veterans on the force. Often the neighborhood he or she patrols for the first time helps to shape the way a rookie works. Patrolman Walter Matthys' first day of patrol was September 7, 1964. As he worked in the neighborhood of Central Avenue and Edythe Street, the eyes of business owners and residents alike smiled as they kept watch over their rookie, welcoming the opportunity to help him along.

Most seasoned officers can recall by name the residents of their post who are a source of trouble, and they know to treat these people with extra caution. In Patrolman Matthys' area, a man known simply as "The King," a recently released mental patient who wore a crown adorned with costume jewelry, was a constant problem. Shortly before one o'clock in the afternoon on September 11, 1964, Patrolman Matthys tried to arrest "The King" at the corner of Central Avenue and Edythe Street for a simple disturbance charge. Matthys seized the deranged man, still wearing his crown of jewels, by the belt to place him under arrest. Then the fight began. The tall, slender, and delusional man grabbed the twenty-one-year-old patrolman around the waist and wrestled him to the ground. Horrified storeowners watched as the young patrolman's revolver was torn from his holster while others rushed to the phone to summon help.

Before assistance could arrive, "the King" fired a series of shots from a department-issue weapon. Arthur Brook, the owner of Brook's Grocery, saw everything. "He took the gun right out of the policeman's holster. . . . He emptied the gun. . . . He kept shooting while he was lying there dead." When he could no longer fire the gun, Cleaven "The King" Dupree simply walked away. Police swarmed the area, and had no trouble locating and arresting Dupree a short distance away. He was still wearing his play crown. They transported their fellow officer, whom they had not had a chance to know, to Church Home and Hospital, where he was pronounced dead from his wounds, after only five days on duty.

The capture of Dupree offered little comfort to Walter's new wife, Shirley Anne. In court, shock was soon compounded by confusion. Onlookers watched in amazement as Dupree was brought before Judge A. Jerome Diener. "The King" appeared to take no interest in the proceedings and lay prostrate on the courtroom floor. Since 1953, Dupree had been arrested forty-three times, served numerous terms in jail for various crimes, and had been committed to and released from the Crownsville State Hospital eleven times. This final act of violence would send Dupree away for the rest of his life.

Patrolman Teddy L. Bafford

October 15, 1964, Northwestern District
11 years, 2 months of service

The night of October 15, 1964, was busy in the Northwestern District. The neighborhood surrounding the 3300 block of Garrison Boulevard was in a state of fear. Gunmen in a green sedan fired wildly at anything or anyone who moved. Residents knew and trusted Officer Teddy Bafford and gave him information about the shooting suspects. Shortly before 10:30 P.M., a couple walking in the neighborhood reported being fired upon. They gave Bafford a very good description, and from the call box at the corner of Garrison Boulevard and Liberty Heights Avenue he relayed this information to police headquarters. Teddy was working on his day off, because he and his wife were preparing for an addition to their family.

Suddenly, he spotted the gunmen. He shouted into the phone that he had the suspects in sight and was going after them. His fellow officers were instructed to respond to the area to assist him. Bafford ran south along Garrison Boulevard, steadily closing the distance between himself and the gunmen. An attendant at a gas station near the call box later stated that he heard three shots, prompting him to run out and see what was happening. He made it out in time to see Patrolman Bafford fall to the ground. Officers swarmed the area. Detectives Walter Crompton and Edward Wisniewski fired at the suspect, Larry Leroy Windsor. No shots hit Windsor, but he fell while running, and several officers jumped onto him and made the arrest.

Patrolman Teddy L. Bafford had served in the United States Marine Corps from March 1949 to March 1952, and had seen combat in Korea. At the time of his death, he was thirty-three years old. He was the father of two boys, Ted and Craig, and his wife, Helen, was pregnant.

Sergeant Jack L. Cooper

December 25, 1964, Northeastern District
17 years of service

The hunt was on for four people wanted in the hold-up of a liquor store in the 2000 block of Greenmount Avenue. During the robbery, which had taken place shortly before 10 P.M. on Christmas Eve, Lt. Joseph T. Maskell had been shot twice while struggling with one of the suspects. Sgt. Jack Cooper met with Patrolmen Charles Kopfelder and Daniel Sobolewski in the 1600 block of Carswell Street at 4:45 A.M. on that cold Christmas morning and gave descriptions of the suspects to his officers before they went their separate ways to continue the search. The officers of the Northeastern District made a pledge to catch those responsible for shooting their Lieutenant.

Seven hours after the robbery, Lieutenant Maskell was in fair condition at St. Joseph's Hospital, and Sergeant Cooper had just stopped a twenty-five-year-old man in the 2600 block of Kennedy Avenue. He had approached a young man and demanded identification. Unknown to Sergeant Cooper, he had stopped the gunman in the liquor store robbery. With the young man's driver's license in his hand, Cooper sat in the car and began to use the radio to run a check. The suspect grew nervous. As the sergeant got out of his car, he met a blast of gunfire.

Patrolmen Kopfelder and Sobolewski heard the shots and rushed toward the scene. When they arrived they found their supervisor lying on the sidewalk ten feet from the open door of his patrol car, bleeding from three fatal wounds. They found the suspect's black leather wallet lying next to Sergeant Cooper's lifeless body and the killer's driver's license on the floor of the patrol car near the clutch pedal. The name on the license was Emanuel Jefferson Veney. At 4:50 A.M. on December 25, 1965, the Baltimore Police Department massed its forces and began an all-out search. Emanuel and his brother Earl would not be on the run for long. Soon they were both in custody and charged with the murder of Sergeant Cooper and the shooting of Lieutenant Maskell. Sergeant Cooper not only served the citizens of Baltimore, but had served his country in the North Atlantic convoy routes with the United States Coast Guard in World War II.

Patrolman Charles R. Ernest

January 20, 1965, Western District
18 years and 1 month of service

At Pearl and Saratoga Streets, Fermon Simon and Louis Owens had a traffic accident. Simon was sitting in traffic when he was jarred by the collision. Owens had run a stop sign, and his 1959 Chevrolet slammed into the rear of Simon's car. Even though their cars were still drivable the two drivers sat blocking traffic. It was fifteen minutes past eleven in the morning on June 13, 1964, and that traffic was relatively heavy. Patrolman Charles Ernest and his partner Joseph Keirle arrived to handle the routine call on the collision. Patrolman Ernest examined the license and other paperwork Simon provided as the two men stood at the heavily damaged rear end of Simon's 1953 Ford.

While they reviewed the circumstances of the accident, Owens was told to back his car away so Keirle could better direct traffic around the scene. Owens took a seat behind the steering wheel, started the engine, and carelessly put the car into gear. But he had not hit reverse, and as he put his foot to the accelerator, the mangled steel and chrome lurched forward. Fermon Simon and Officer Ernest were powerless to stop it and in an instant were pinned between the two cars. Owens immediately backed his car away, but the damage had been done. When released from the steel trap, Patrolman Ernest dropped to the ground in terrible pain. The collision had shattered the hips of both men. Patrolman Keirle called for an ambulance and did his best to make them comfortable. The crew of Ambulance #1 sped them to University Hospital.

The hospital staff summoned Dr. John O'Connor, the official departmental doctor, to care for the injured officer. After days of treatment and surgery, O'Connor determined that Charles needed long-term care and assigned Dr. Edward Wenzlaff as his primary physician. When the immediate danger to his health had passed, Charles was taken to his home with hopes of recovery. With his wife Dorothy and daughter Marie caring for him constantly, he never had a shortage of visitors. Unfortunately, hopes waned with the steady decline in his condition. Even though he had the benefit of an assigned departmental physician, he did not progress the way his doctor hoped. On January 20, 1965, after 221 days of bed rest at his home, he suffered a severe heart attack as a result of the initial injuries and died.

Charles Ernest was a well-respected sergeant in the army during World War II and had faced the dangers of combat for nearly two years. He spent almost half of his life in the Western District and faced its danger there every day. In 1960, he had been awarded a commendation for confronting an armed man and trading shots with him. The veteran officer was never cavalier about dangerous situations, and it was his keen sense of area awareness that had kept him safe. He never could have suspected that a call for a simple traffic accident would cause his death.

PATROLMAN ROBERT H. KUHN

July 22, 1965, Western District
1 year and 1 month of service

Robert Kuhn kept a newspaper clipping in his hat that told the account of Patrolman Walter Matthys' death. Kuhn and Matthys had attended the police academy together and his friend's death had had a profound effect on him. Matthys had worked the street only five days before being shot to death with his own revolver by a mentally deranged man named Cleaven Dupree. Kuhn and Matthys had shared many things in common: both were young, newly married, and members of the armed services. Kuhn, an active reservist in the United States Marine Corps, was also expecting his first child with his wife Carla. Hardly a day went by that Robert did not think of his friend and the horrible way in which he had died.

Just after one o'clock on a warm July morning only ten months after Walter Matthys' death, Patrolman Kuhn noticed a black and white convertible double-parked in the 3100 block of West North Avenue, across the street from the firehouse. He went to the driver's side door and spoke with David Cooper to see if anything was amiss. Cooper was with his nephew William, and after some questioning, Kuhn decided that there was nothing to pursue and began to walk away. David Cooper felt otherwise. Believing that Kuhn had slighted him in some way, Cooper got out of the car and boldly shot Kuhn in the back with a .32 caliber pistol. Kuhn fell to the ground in pain.

The shot drew the attention of Fireman Carlos Downs, who was in the firehouse across the street. He rushed out to see Cooper firing shot after shot into Patrolman Kuhn's body. Cooper then jumped into the convertible with his nephew and drove off. Fireman Downs crossed the street to find the officer in a semi-conscious state and non-communicative. "He just moaned, and he kept moaning until we tried to put him in the ambulance. Then there was no sound at all," said Downs. News of the shooting traveled quickly, and police, using the description provided by Downs, found Cooper only minutes later.

As the two drove away from the scene, Cooper and his nephew argued vehemently. Cooper then shot William three times in the head with a .22 caliber handgun, apparently because he refused to cooperate or help the killer. Cooper parked the car and began walking. Patrolmen John Hess and James Griffin confronted him in the 1600 block of St. Stephens Street. Cooper threw his arms into the air, revealing the .22 caliber gun in his waistband. Griffin grabbed the gun and Cooper immediately tried to get it back. "I shot that police and I'll kill all of you," Cooper screamed as he fought the two officers. When he could not regain control of his own gun, he went for Patrolman Hess' service weapon. Fortunately, Hess and Griffin gained control of the murderer, subduing him with their nightsticks.

Because of the violent struggle, Cooper was transported to Lutheran Hospital in an ambulance. As he rode he kicked and punched Patrolman Robert Powell in the face. Upon arrival at the hospital, officers and medical staff used leather straps and handcuffs to restrain the man. At five minutes after three in the morning of July 22, 1965, Cooper spoke his final words. "I shot my nephew because he wasn't with me. He was going to leave me. . . . We fought." Then he died of a heart attack. Later it was learned that Cooper had been discharged from military service after being diagnosed with a mental disorder. Once out of the military he had been arrested several times for narcotics violations.

Patrolman Robert Kuhn had emulated his father. For thirty-five years, Frank W. Kuhn Sr. had served the citizens of the Baltimore City. For twenty-seven of those years he rode horseback through the streets and carried the pride of his young son with him. In the short time of Robert's service he had already gained the notice of the higher commanders. His District Captain spoke highly of him and often said that he was "a good policeman with the potentials of an excellent policeman."

Patrolman William J. Baumer

January 25, 1967, Eastern District
20 years of service

On Saturday, January 28, 1967, Patrolman William Baumer's friends, family, and fellow officers gathered at the Sacred Heart Catholic Church at 600 South Conkling Street to say goodbye. William had spent all of his life within this tight East Baltimore community, with the exception of serving his country in the U.S. Army during World War II. A graduate of Patterson Park High School, who had joined the Baltimore Police Department at the age of twenty-nine, he knew the importance of maintaining order and peace in and around the homes and businesses near Patterson Park.

Patrolman Baumer was walking outside Gordon's Sub Shop, at the corner of Orleans Street and Patterson Park Avenue, when he noticed James Streeter Jr. screaming at the storeowner and refusing to leave. Taking control of Streeter, a person nearly thirty years his junior, he began walking to the nearest call box to call for a wagon. The young man was angry at being arrested and resisted Patrolman Baumer's attempts to control him. As they neared the call box, the young man struggled to break free. Baumer crumpled to the ground, and Streeter ran for his freedom. Citizens watching the altercation had no idea why the officer had fallen to the ground but felt duty-bound to chase Streeter down. Not a hundred feet from the call box Harvey Dawson and William Pennington tackled the young man as he ran and held him until Patrolmen Robert Rubin and Donald Martin arrived. Help was called, but it was too late.

When Patrolman William Baumer reached Church Home and Hospital in eastern Baltimore, he was pronounced dead of a heart attack. At his home at 2405 Fleet Street, his family tried to console themselves. At the time of his death he was unmarried and without children. What he did have were his two sisters, Margaret and Barbara; brothers, John and Germanus; and the support and appreciation of a very grateful community for such long service.

Patrolman Frederick K. Kontner

February 10, 1967, Northern District
6 years and 11 months of service

Despite the strong recommendation of a staff psychiatrist at the Patuxent Institution, Donald Leo Sabutas was released from his treatment and set free onto the streets of Baltimore. Not only did Sabutas's diminished mental capacity present something of a danger to the public, he possessed criminal tendencies as well. One of the first things Sabutas decided to do was join the drug culture. Looking for drugs to buy, he approached several men standing on North Avenue at Guilford.

An alert officer, Frederick Kontner, and his partner Officer Raymond Tartel spotted these men and knew from experience that they were involved in buying and selling drugs. They pulled up to the corner and got out of their car to get the identification of the men and possibly arrest them. As they got out of their patrol car, Donald Sabutas ran from the officers. Officer Tartel stayed with the men on North Avenue as Officer Kontner pursued Sabutas.

The two men ran north on Guilford Avenue. Sabutas made an abrupt turn on East 23rd Street and then turned again into an alley. Officer Kontner was close behind. As he rounded the corner and entered the alley he encountered gunfire. Sabutas had taken cover behind a parked car filled with eight innocent passengers. Officer Kontner fell to the ground mortally wounded but still able to return fire. Sabutas continued shooting, also striking a thirteen-year-old boy in the arm. Soon, backup officers arrived, and Sabutas fled again.

Eventually, he was cornered and gunned down in a volley of police gunfire behind the State Office Building in the 2100 block of Guilford Avenue, now the Parole and Probation Building.

Officer Kontner was active in the Marine Corps Reserves and left behind his wife, Mary Lou.

Patrolman John C. Williams

August 21, 1967, Northern District
6 years of service

Landmarks have often offered considerable symbolism in their design and function. In 1899 the Baltimore Police Department completed the construction of one of its most impressive and eye-catching structures. Built at a time when attention to detail came second only to architectural inspiration, the Northern District station represented protection to the proud neighborhood of Hampden. At the corner of Keswick and 34th Streets, the granite, brick and brownstone building, designed by Henry Braums in the French-Renaissance style, rose well above the surrounding houses. The view from the roof of the station house has seen considerable change as the city's characteristic skyline grew from that of a brawling port to one befitting a busy, modern city. The officers who have worked in this magnificent building share a special pride that has followed to their new station, built more than a hundred years later.

To look around inside the yard of the old district was to see the shadows of history. The iron gates that closed off the entrance were left open once the stables that housed the department's horses were no longer needed. The wide-open yard was once the scene of work-out sessions for police, and training exercises to teach officers better methods of crowd control and self-defense. Until the gates were shut permanently, officers found ways to use the yard for recreation as well as a place to park police cars. When the day came to finally clear out the station, officers removed everything from barbeque grills to motorcycles.

Patrolman John Williams spent thirteen years in the Baltimore Park Police prior to joining the police department and enjoyed his assignment to the Northern District. At 7:15 on the morning on June 27, 1967, he sat in the passenger seat of Radio Car #505, a 1967 Chevrolet Belair, writing reports. It was the end of his tour of duty and he and his partner, Patrolman Walter Stahl, were making sure that the oncoming shift would have a fully fueled car. Walter parked next to the gas pumps inside the station house yard and waited while Patrolman John Harvey filled the vehicle.

Something sparked and ignited the fuel, and the car was instantly engulfed in flames. The initial blast blew Harvey backward, away from the heat and fire. Stahl jumped from the driver's seat and watched as his partner tried to escape. When Williams stepped from the patrol car, his foot splashed down into burning gasoline. He was surrounded by fire, but help was immediate. His partners extinguished the flames as fast as they could. Medic 11 responded and transported John to Union Memorial Hospital's Burn Unit, where they found first, second, and third degree burns over almost half of his body. Still, Dr. Fred Cole expected that John would be in the hospital only two weeks. The injuries, though, were more severe than the doctor initially thought. Eight weeks later, on August 21, 1967, Patrolman John Williams died as the result of his injuries.

When he died, John was forty-nine years old. In addition to his combined nineteen years of policing, he had served in the army during World War II in the 110th Field Artillery Battalion and the 735th

Police Battalion in North Africa and Europe. Once he finished his military service, he returned to Baltimore to marry Rosina and father a daughter, named for her mother.

Detective Richard F. Bosak

April 18, 1968, Criminal Investigation Division, 16 years and 3 months of service

James V. Galliard planned his escape from the city jail around an upcoming doctor's appointment. As an armed guard walked Galliard to the appointment, a young woman bumped into the pair and passed a pistol to the convicted narcotics user. Galliard wheeled, fired several shots at the guard, and ran away. The guard, unhurt, gave chase but soon lost sight of him. The escape called for the attention of the best detectives the city had to offer. The task fell into the hands of Homicide Detective Richard Bosak.

On April 18, 1968, Detective Bosak received a tip that Galliard was going to meet a friend at the Golden Glow Restaurant in the unit block of North Eutaw Street. Galliard was armed with the same gun he had used to shoot his way to freedom the previous Wednesday. Minutes before 6 P.M., Detective Bosak along with the bar owner and another officer, emerged from the kitchen to trap the suspect. Galliard and his friend attempted to flee by running for the front door. Bosak was faster. The detective tackled Galliard just before he made it out of the bar.

The men wrestled furiously, one fighting for his freedom, the other fighting to protect himself and innnocent citizens from harm.

Suddenly the fight ended in gunfire. People watched in horror as Detective Bosak slumped to the floor, mortally wounded. Galliard ripped the detective's revolver from his holster and ran from the scene. Bosak's partner followed closely behind and cornered Galliard in the nearby Hecht Company parking lot. Faced with his imminent capture, Galliard raised his pistol to his head and pulled the trigger, killing himself instantly.

Patrolman George F. Heim

January 16, 1970, Southeastern District
17 years and 4 months of service

The families and friends of police officers know their loved ones face danger in all sorts of environments and from all kinds of people. When thoughts of these dangers come to mind, they usually involve criminals with guns, or acts of selfless heroism to save the lives of others. Unfortunately, the simple danger of being in and around automobile traffic has been responsible for the deaths of many officers nationwide. That danger increases during inclement weather, and when inexperienced or negligent drivers are on the road. Police officers do not have a choice when it comes to their working conditions. They are responsible for safeguarding life and property regardless of the elements. So it was at nine o'clock on the morning of January 16, 1970.

When a fellow officer called for assistance in dealing with heavy traffic around an accident scene, Patrolman George Heim answered the call, making his way through a nearly blinding snowstorm to the

5600 block of O'Donnell Street. A seasoned veteran, he was well aware of the danger that surrounds officers as they try to handle accident scenes in heavy snow. In order to appropriately guard against other vehicles traveling in the area, Patrolman Heim went to the trunk of his patrol car to retrieve some flares.

He never had a chance to light those flares. A car that had gone out of control was headed his way. Heavy snow and the speed of the approaching automobile combined to prevent any chance of escape. Robert Bryant was driving too fast for conditions and barely able to see in front of him because of heavy salt deposits on his windshield. His car slid into the helpless policeman, inflicting fatal internal injuries. An investigation later determined that Bryant was operating his car with gross negligence, and he was charged with causing the death of Patrolman Heim.

His supervisors described George Heim as a man both honest and pleasant to be around, who had a special knack for police work. George was forty-one years old when he died, and he left behind his wife Rosemary, daughter Mrs. Rosemary Goodnow, and son, George Jr.

PATROLMAN HENRY M. MICKEY

March 24, 1970, Central District
10 months of service

Henry Mickey and his partners, Patrolmen Victor Dennis and Vincent Cole made their way to the rear of a rowhouse in the 1800 block of Pennsylvania Avenue. It was ten minutes before 11 P.M., on March 24, 1970, and the three plainclothes policemen took care not to alert the man they had come to arrest. Armed with a warrant for a narcotics violation, they climbed the stairway to James Stewart's second floor apartment that sat above a shoe store. Because of the narrow stairway, the officers had to stand in front of the door as they knocked and announced their presence.

Stewart, like many involved in the drug trade, was a violent man who always had a firearm within reach. Surprised by the officers, but not unprepared for a confrontation, he grabbed a rifle and opened the door. Patrolman Mickey stood directly in his line of sight when the light from the apartment illuminated him. Stewart fired a single shot from his rifle, which struck Mickey squarely in the chest and killed him instantly. Patrolmen Dennis and Cole immediately returned fire with their revolvers, killing Stewart.

Now Dennis and Cole had to focus on a new and very dangerous situation. They did not know if any others were inside the apartment who might pose a threat. After seeing their friend shot dead, they had to enter the residence immediately and make certain that they too did not become victims of violence. In a move that possibly saved their lives, they made their way tactically inside and cleared the cramped apartment. Once inside they found a second man, Richard Tune, in hiding. They arrested him and secured the scene.

Patrolman Henry Mickey and James Stewart were pronounced dead when they arrived at Providence Hospital. Henry Mickey had less than a year of experience with the Baltimore Police Department, but his professionalism and proficiency had led to his appointment to the plainclothes drug unit. Henry was twenty-eight years old at the time of his death and left his wife, Frances, and a stepson, Damon. While his immediate family was small, he was one of five brothers and two sisters.

Patrolman Donald W. Sager

April 24, 1970, Central District
17 years of service

In the first four months of 1970, the Baltimore City Police Department was rocked by the sudden loss of three officers. Exactly one month prior to April 24, Patrolman Henry M. Mickey had been gunned down on Pennsylvania Avenue, leaving the officers of the Central District more than usually protective of each other. But even though the danger of violence against them is ever-present, police officers still have a responsibility to help the public.

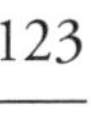

At twenty minutes after nine on the evening of April 24, 1970, a young woman called for police help when her drunken, estranged husband began arguing with her. Patrolman Donald Sager was called to the house, in the 1200 block of Myrtle Avenue, for a domestic disturbance, and Stanley Sierakowski responded eagerly as a backup unit.

By the time they arrived, the husband had left. The two officers spent time with the woman, assuring her that she was safe, and did their best to provide information on how to protect herself in the future. Nearly fifty minutes had passed before the two officers decided to leave. They walked to Sager's car and sat to talk for a while. Donald went to the driver's side and got behind the wheel, while Stanley sat sideways in the passenger seat, resting his feet on the curb. Sager began to make notes in order to complete a report.

Unbeknownst to them, James Edward Powell and Jack I. Johnson, both armed with pistols, were creeping silently toward them. The pair made their way close to the patrol vehicle, and, for no other reason than the fact that Sager and Sierakowski were police officers, opened fire. Glass flew as the car's windows shattered. As quickly as it had begun, the ambush ended. Donald Sager was killed instantly by a gunshot wound to the head, and Stanley Sierakowski fell to the ground with wounds to the stomach and arms. At 9:57 P.M. a single broadcast by Sierakowski came over police radios throughout the city. "I am shot in front of 1201 Myrtle Avenue." All who heard took instant action. Within minutes the area was saturated with officers and detectives and a thorough search had begun.

Radio calls gave responding officers descriptions and possible escape routes to check. Every officer summoned his utmost strength and resolve. The men and women of the Baltimore Police began a systematic search of the immediate area. Officers crashed into vacant houses and searched them. The fire department used a powerful searchlight to check the rooftops of the neighborhood. Powell and Johnson were found hiding beneath porches nearby and arrested. Stanley was taken to Maryland General Hospital where his wife, Florence, joined him. Despite the seriousness of his wounds, Stanley's primary concern was that of his partner Donald. Quite some time would pass before Stanley was told of his friend's death.

Patrolman Sager was the third officer killed in the line of duty in the first four months of 1970. This tragic series of events was the beginning of the most violent decade in the history of the department, one in which twenty officers would lose their lives.

Patrolman Carl Peterson, Jr.

June 12, 1971, Central District
20 years and 5 months of service

On the night of June 12, 1971, Officer Carl Peterson was using a call box at the corner of Lexington and Greene Streets late in his shift. In two hours he was going to be on his way home. He was known as "Officer Pete," or simply "Pete," to citizens and his fellow police officers alike. His love for his job was often evident when he gave candy to the local children. But tonight, the father of one of those children, Roland Jackson, saw an opportunity to ambush Officer Peterson. Without warning, Jackson struck Officer Peterson as he was using the call box, knocking him to the ground.

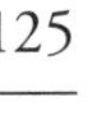

Jackson pulled Officer Peterson's revolver from his holster, stood over him, and fired one shot into the helpless officer's head, inflicting a mortal wound. With no witnesses to this crime, Officer Peterson's death went unreported for several minutes until a passerby noticed him lying on the sidewalk. It is unclear why Roland Jackson murdered Officer Peterson, but what he did immediately following this deplorable act is almost as puzzling. He ran from the scene, forced his way into 239 N. Pearl Street, and took a helpless, two-year-old girl as a hostage. Officers responding to the call for a hostage situation were unaware of Peterson's death, as were his side partners. Nor could they know that as he lay dead on the street, his service weapon was being held to a child's head.

Officers Kenneth Burke and Arnold Adams responded to the call and acted decisively. Residents of the neighborhood reported to the officers that they had seen Jackson, carrying a revolver and a young girl, kick in the front door of 239 and enter the residence. Fearing for the life of the child, Burke and Adams decided they had to go in after him. Adams, carrying a shotgun, led the two-man team. Encountering residents as they made their way through the house, they finally came to the door behind which Jackson was hiding. Jackson refused to obey the officers' commands to lay down his weapon and surrender. They took a deep breath and kicked in the door of the third floor apartment.

Face to face with Jackson, and staring down the barrel of the service revolver that had just killed his friend, Adams could not pull the trigger of his shotgun because the small child was in the line of fire. Adams retreated to the safety of the hallway. Jackson went after him, grabbing the barrel of the shotgun, and the fight was on. Jackson managed to create distance between them and leveled the sights of the pistol at Officer Burke. Burke seized the gun and fired his own weapon but missed. Through sheer will and power, Officers Burke and Adams eventually arrested Jackson without further loss of life.

While Burke and Adams were involved in their own life-and-death struggle, Officer Bruce Green met a frantic citizen, Alvin Gill, who reported that an officer had been shot and was lying wounded at the corner of Lexington and Pearle Streets. Green summoned help, and an ambulance arrived to take the wounded man to University Hospital. At 11:45 P.M., Dr. Daniel Cook of the Neurological Staff, pronounced Officer Peterson dead.

Only after Officers Burke and Adams survived their own perilous struggle would they discover that they had arrested the man who had stolen the life of their friend and partner, "Pete." Unfortunately, tragedy continued to stalk the Peterson family following Carl's death. His wife, Helen, grieved openly but found strength in her daughter and son-in-law. They spent time together and made the sad decisions regarding Carl's arrangements. Yet only two days after they had selected the headstone for the gravesite, the final detail for the funeral, Helen died of a massive heart attack.

Lieutenant Martin E. Webb

August 1, 1971, Southern District
17 years of service

On the morning of August 2, 1971, officeres of the Baltimore County Police Department found a car, with all of its doors open and no owner or operator in sight, just outside of the northeast section of Baltimore City. What made this discovery still more unusual was that it occurred just after torrential storms had moved through the area, causing dangerous flash flooding. Investigation by the county officers would reveal the most disturbing discovery of the day: the abandoned car belonged to Lt. Martin E. Webb of the Baltimore City Police Department. Initial attempts to locate the Lieutenant were unsuccessful.

Shortly after the investigation began, the terrible circumstances surrounding Lieutenant Webb's death became clear. Several witnesses were found who described his last heroic actions. While driving home during the storms, Lieutenant Webb had come across a woman trapped inside her overturned vehicle and in imminent danger of drowning in the rising floodwaters. Bound by a sense of duty, Lieutenant Webb made his way to her and saved the woman's life, only to lose his own when the strong currents overtook him. Lt. Donald Sutton and twelve volunteer officers formed a search party and found his body nearly half a mile away in Kahler's Run.

Under the Good Samaritan Law, Police Officers nationwide are bound, whether on or off-duty, to act in defense of life when it is threatened. Once officers act in a life-saving capacity, they place themselves in an on-duty status. But because of the type of people who are drawn to the profession of law enforcement, no law is necessary. Time after time history has shown that officers are willing to place themselves in danger in order to protect the lives of others. In a Baltimore City police newsletter, Lieutenant Webb was remembered as a person who "did not hesitate to risk his life in order to save the life of another. His tragic death was the direct result of the compassion and concern he held for his fellow man, a dedication commensurate with the esteem in which his memory will forever be held." Lieutenant Webb left his wife Frances and two children.

PATROLMAN LORENZO A. GRAY

July 26, 1972, Southeastern District
2 years and 6 months of service

The American military sometimes did its best to accommodate service members during the years of conflict in Vietnam. Lorenzo Gray was serving his country as a U.S. Marine in the Southeast Asian country when he received news that his mother had died. Arrangements were quickly made and the young Marine was sent home to care for his three stepsisters and two step brothers. The cramped rowhouse depended on Lorenzo for its income, so to provide for his large family he joined the Baltimore Police Department in February 1969 and took a second job as a taxicab driver. When help was needed,

Lorenzo was there. Not merely a provider for his family or a protector of his city, he also took on the added responsibility of helping to raise the children of Mrs. Beatrice Brooks. "He was just like a brother. He used to come and check on me while I was working," she said. She also said that on many occasions he served as the father figure for her children. "He disciplines them and makes sure they do the right thing."

His giving nature and dedication to do what was right put him in the line of fire in defense of his country and in defense of the citizens of Baltimore. On the evening of July 25, 1972, he patrolled the streets around the 3600 block of Pulaski Highway, keeping a sharp eye for anyone doing wrong. In Beatrice Brooks's loving words, "He was bitterly against crime. Major or minor crime it didn't matter. He was bitterly against all crime." Earlier in the evening, the employees of a convenience store at the corner of Highland Avenue and Fayette Street had been the victims of an armed robbery. Although the area was not on his post, he made it his business to do what he could to bring to justice those who were responsible for such a violent crime. At 10:30 in the evening he and Patrolman William Heath were standing in front of the Holiday Inn, when a frantic employee ran up to them. The excited man quickly conveyed to the two officers that another robbery was in progress at that very moment.

Heath and Gray did not hesitate but ran inside a rear entrance to the kitchen where they encountered two armed men. Heath tackled the first man, Robert Lee Wilson, who was armed with a .38 caliber handgun. The men battled on the floor for the weapon. Heath quickly gained control of Wilson, and Gray pursued the other man as he ran into the dining room. But when Gray burst through the swinging kitchen door, he saw George Molburn aiming his sawed-off shotgun at him. There was nowhere to go, no cover available, and no time to close the distance. Lorenzo Gray drew his weapon and fired at the same time Molburn squeezed the trigger on his shotgun. The blast knocked Lorenzo back through the swinging doors and onto the floor, and left him mortally wounded in the chest. Heath maintained control of Wilson and called for backup. Fortunately, federal narcotic agents were conducting surveillance on certain guests in the hotel and helped to capture Molburn. Patrolman Gray and his assailant were transported to the Johns Hopkins Hospital for treatment. In the exchange of fire, Gray's only shot had found its mark in Molburn's back.

Molburn would recover from his wounds, but Gray would not. At 1:30 on the morning of July 26, 1972, Lorenzo Gray died on an operating table as doctors worked to save him. He was an important facet in many lives, described as "one of America's sons" and "a soldier in two wars." Lorenzo Gray had taken on great responsibilities for family, community, and nation, and he did it without complaint. He was a proud father of two girls, Audra and Angela, and a loving member of a huge family.

Patrolman Robert M. Hurley

March 29, 1973, Northeastern District
16 years and 6 months of service

Constantinos Courtalis shut the door of his business and walked his sister-in-law, Penny, to her car in the parking lot. He carefully shut the driver's side door, for she was four months pregnant. Then he noticed a car erratically traveling south on Erdman Avenue from Sinclair Lane, a 1972 Chevrolet Impala, swerving and apparently out of control. It leapt over a curb, struck a light pole, and careened through a low shrub, heading straight for Penny's car. Constantinos called out to Penny to warn her, then got behind a strong sign support pole. When the Chevy came to rest, Constantinos ran to Penny's side. She was in pain but not injured badly.

Constantinos heard cries for help coming from Mrs. Angelina Hurley in the Chevy, and he made his way to her side as well. Mrs. Hurley knew her husband, Robert, was in serious trouble. Moments earlier, just before the crash, Robert had grabbed his chest in pain and lost control of his car. Soon after, help came in the form of an ambulance and several police officers. Those who arrived on the scene immediately recognized Robert as one of their own, an officer from the Northeastern District, who had been involved in a serious crash while on duty the day before. With so many life-threatening situations, the rescuers worked feverishly to provide aid to Robert, his wife, and the young pregnant woman. Robert and Penny were both transported to the Johns Hopkins Hospital.

Penny escaped with minor bruises, but Robert was pronounced dead at the scene. It was quickly discovered that he had an extensive history of worsening heart disease that was one of the major contributors to his death. His partners on the force and his family asserted that his death was the result of his line-of-duty accident the day before, when his attempt to apprehend a criminal fleeing by car ended in a major collision. At the time, Robert had complained of chest pain, and at the end of his tour of duty he had gone home to rest. Nevertheless, at first the heart attack was not considered to be line-of-duty related.

After an exhaustive investigation and the affirmation by Dr. Albert Antlitz that the car chase the day before his death was "vigorous and had to be associated with marked stress and strain both physical and emotional," his death was ruled as having occurred in the line of duty. His fellow officers knew Robert Hurley as a man who did a very professional job and did it without complaint. Even though he experienced the pain and discomfort associated with a heart condition, he went to work with the goal of being there when his side partners needed him. Because of that drive, he was involved in the crash that would cause his death. He had the love and support of his wife Angelina and the respect of his son, Robert Jr. Eventually his son would answer the call to serve his community as a police officer as well, and join the Maryland Transportation Authority Police.

PATROLMAN NORMAN F. BUCHMAN

April 6, 1973, Northwestern District
3 years and 9 months of service

Greenspring Avenue winds up and down a large hill with twists and turns that make even the best cars lean wildly from side to side. yet Patrolman Norman Buchman kept pace with the Lincoln Continental driven by a wanted man as the two cars sped down the notoriously treacherous stretch of road south of Cold Spring Lane. On this early spring day, the patrolman spotted the known criminal, Michael Sean Garland, in the Northwestern District and the car chase began. The two large cars roared across the district boundaries and eventually past Northern District Patrolmen Jerome Chambers and John Cullings, who joined the pursuit. As quickly as they joined the chase, Chambers and Cullings lost sight of Buchman.

The two Northern District officers correctly figured that Buchman's suspect had turned westbound back toward the northwest Baltimore neighborhood where the chase had begun. The streets onto which they turned were crowded with parked cars. After several turns, the chase came to a stop in the middle of the 2500 block of Quantico Avenue. Buchman jumped out to apprehend Garland before he could run. Garland had decided that he was not going to simply fight for his freedom; he was going to take the officer's life. He wrestled Buchman to the ground and ripped the twenty-four-year-old patrolman's service revolver from its holster.

Garland fired every round from the revolver into the body of Patrolman Buchman as he lay on the ground, killing him. The gunfire drew the attention of Chambers and Cullings as they canvassed the neighborhood for a sign of the chase they had lost. As they rounded a corner, they confronted Garland at the bloody scene, took him into custody immediately, and found the dead patrolman's gun only a few feet from his body.

Buchman was a decorated veteran of Vietnam, where he had served as a combat photographer. He had received a purple heart for a wound incurred while taking a picture of what he thought was a dead enemy soldier. As he stared through the camera, the severely wounded man pulled the pin on a grenade. When it detonated, flying shrapnel wounded him in the shoulder. He came home from that conflict, only to go back into battle on the streets of Baltimore. Patrolman Buchman left behind a young wife, Cheryl, and their two-year-old daughter, Jennifer.

After Lorenzo Gray's death in 1972 and Patrolman Buchman's death on Quantico Avenue, each leaving young families with no financial support, Mayor William Donald Schaefer established a "Fallen Heroes Children's Fund."

Patrolman Calvin M. Rodwell

September 22, 1973, Southeastern District
12 years of service

Like many officers, Patrolman Calvin Rodwell knew that presenting children with a positive image of police officers is of paramount importance. To that end he sought assignments within the department that allowed him to spend time teaching children and building a foundation of trust in young minds. Officer Rodwell's dedication to children went far beyond the eight-hour workday. In addition to teaching traffic safety at "Safety City" in the Southeastern District, he volunteered as an assistant scoutmaster at a local Boy Scout Troop, and served with the Big Brothers of Baltimore. In his official position, he rarely confronted violent suspects.

To make ends meet, Calvin moonlighted as a taxi driver. That was not unusual; off-duty officers often worked as cabbies, and the department gave its blessing to this type of work for it helped stem the rising tide of violent crimes against cab drivers. Shortly after midnight on Friday, September 21, 1973, Officer Rodwell picked up a fare at the corner of McCullough and Wilson Streets. Louis Walker got into the back of Calvin's cab and requested a trip to Orleans and Aisquith Streets. Calvin quickly guided his cab through the empty streets. As they neared the intersection, Walker suddenly produced a gun and forced Calvin to pull to the curb, where Walker ordered him out of the cab. Walker drove away with more than the officer's cab and money—the officer's gun lay beneath a cushion on the driver's seat. Rodwell pursued on foot but soon lost sight of the cab. Several things Calvin could not have known stacked the odds against him that night. The gun used to rob him was borrowed. Walker had gotten the pistol from a cabbie by the name of Ridgley Young. He had been on the way to return it to Young when he hailed Rodwell's cab.

Rodwell spotted a cab and ran toward it for help. It was none other than Young's taxi, and as Rodwell neared it, he had no way of knowing that Walker, who had met up with Young and returned the pistol, was in the back seat. Walker got out of the cab and confronted the policeman. Witnesses heard Rodwell plead for his life moments before three shots were fired. Two struck their target. Officers and medics dispatched to the scene rushed the wounded man to Church Home and Hospital, where he was pronounced dead after midnight on Saturday, September 22.

Calvin Rodwell had touched the lives of many children during his twelve years of service, and sadly he would leave behind his wife, Dorothy and three children Kimberly, Andre, and Dino. Shortly after the shooting, Walker was arrested and charged with the murder of this devoted family man and role model.

Patrolman Frank W. Whitby, Jr.

May 5, 1974, Eastern District
1 year and 7 months of service

Despite their outward similarity, Baltimore's rowhouses are filled with unique features. Most have beautiful hardwood floors and extensive molding that builders took special care to craft. With all the effort spent to make the living spaces as large as possible, the hallways are characteristically narrow. It is rare to find in a Baltimore rowhouse a hallway wide enough for two adults to walk side by side. In one instance, this constricted space would save the life of one officer and contribute to another's death.

Early on the afternoon of April 6, 1974, exactly one year after the brutal slaying of Patrolman Norman Buchman, two Eastern District officers, Frank Whitby and Carl Grinnage, answered the call for a man shooting wildly in the 1900 block of East Lanvale Street. Because both had worked in the Eastern District, they had routinely answered the call for people discharging firearms. More often than not, these calls turned out to be unfounded, but on this particular day, Luke James had actually been firing a handgun into the air. When they arrived on East Lanvale Street, Whitby and Grinnage learned that the fifty-two-year-old James was at his sister's house, hiding. The two officers decided to go inside and arrest him. Whitby retrieved the shotgun from the trunk of his patrol car and led the way into the house.

As soon as the officers entered, they found themselves in a narrow hallway fourteen feet long. It was dangerous and difficult to move under these circumstances, and both men kept their eyes open for the gunman. Suddenly, at the other end of the hallway, James appeared and began firing. Whitby and Grinnage were trapped. The first of James's bullets ripped through Whitby as the policemen sought cover, but because the corridor was so narrow, the only avenue of escape was retreat. Whitby made the supreme sacrifice, protecting his partner by shoving Grinnage out through the door to safety while shielding him with his body. Whitby dropped the shotgun as the officers backed their way down the corridor and out the door. James advanced and picked it up.

The injured Whitby called for help and took cover with Grinnage. When backup officers arrived, they discovered that James not only had Whitby's shotgun, he had barricaded himself inside with a ten-year-old girl. Luke James, drunk and realizing there was no way out, soon surrendered to negotiators. He was handcuffed but refused to walk to the wagon. Officers now had to deal with a man who threw himself on the ground and yelled continuously in front of a large crowd that had gathered to watch. Witnesses told officers that James had been drinking throughout the day at a bar called Lottie's Club, around the corner from the scene of the shooting. Further investigation revealed that James was a repeat offender for charges such as armed robbery, and had served fourteen years in a state penitentiary.

Frank Whitby was taken immediately to the Johns Hopkins Hospital, where he underwent surgery. After five hours of operating, doctors described his condition as "near death" but alive. As the days passed, Frank's condition improved slightly, but then it turned for the worse. A month later, on May 5, 1974, at 7:05 A.M., the twenty-two-year-old Frank Whitby, husband of Elizabeth and father of three-year-old Dorothy and five-month-old Frances, died of a pulmonary infection caused by the wounds.

Detective Sergeant Frank W. Grunder, Jr.

August 1, 1974, Escape and Apprehension Unit, 12 years of service

Ronald Johnson was riding his motorcycle when he began having mechanical problems at the corner of Harford Road and Echodale Avenue. He pulled the bike to the curb and attempted to repair the malfunction. Several minutes passed while he tried to get the vehicle road-worthy, and he grew increasingly frustrated. Rather than push the bike to a nearby shop, he decided to catch the next bus home and return with tools to make the job easier. As he sat and waited, he kept the pistol he was wearing concealed from the public's watchful eyes. Johnson was not a man who followed the straight and narrow; he preyed on others to support himself and had numerous felony arrests dating back to 1960. The twenty-nine-year-old Johnson was a bank robber and, until August 1, 1974, a successful one.

Johnson, an ex-convict from the West Coast with stolen money in his pockets, sat on the steps of St. Dominic's Roman Catholic Church and patiently waited for his bus, unaware that detectives from the citywide robbery unit were closing in on him. Despite having received a credible tip about Johnson, they had spent that Thursday night staking out the area's banks in an attempt to catch him in the act. The local newspapers had enlisted the help of citizens by publishing pictures of the bank robber and pleading for information. It was one of these pictures that enabled Detective Sergeant Frank Grunder to spot the wanted man.

The head of the Escapee and Apprehension Unit, Frank Grunder had an excellent memory for faces. Whether from innate ability or a skill acquired by the demands of his position, Frank Grunder could simply glance at a person and not only recognize him but remember the crime for which he was wanted. On this day, as he was driving down Harford Road with his family, his ability came to good use. His wife Beverly, sons Frank and Mark, and daughter Beth were with him when, just before eight in the evening he spotted Johnson sitting on the steps of St. Dominic's. Frank knew how dangerous this man was and parked a safe distance away, telling his family to stay in the car. He could not waste the opportunity to catch a man holding area businesses in fear, so he started to walk to a nearby phone to call for on-duty officers to help. At that moment Officer Joseph L. Shaw of the Northeastern District drove by. The sergeant waved him down.

Shaw, a rookie with only six months of experience, was excited to help and walked slightly behind the sergeant as they approached the wanted man. Frank pulled his badge from his pocket and identified himself. The startled criminal started to run but only far enough that he could withdraw his pistol. He turned, crouched into a shooting position, and took aim. Surprised by the move, Sergeant Grunder could not get off a clean shot as the criminal turned on him. Johnson fired, and his bullet struck Frank in the chest. Shaw fared better and was able to shoot down the murderer. Frank Grunder's wife and children turned fearfully toward the sound of the shooting. In the aftermath, they watched Reverend Thomas Ryan of St. Dominic's kneel over their husband and father, offering up the sacrament of Last Rites. The wounded sergeant later died at Union Memorial Hospital.

On August 5, 1974, Detective Sergeant Frank Grunder's life was celebrated at his funeral. Memories were shared and stories told about his devotion to family and his ability to do a tough job and do it well. Inside St. Dominic's Church, a few yards from the scene of the crime just four days past, the thirty-four-year-old sergeant lay in his coffin, his family around him.

Patrolman Milton I. Spell

August 15, 1974, Eastern District
6 years and 9 months of service

Milton Spell's decision to become a police officer came after he had spent three tours of duty with the Special Forces in Vietnam. His service record was exemplary. Although the standard tour of duty in Vietnam was only a year or in some cases thirteen months, he volunteered to stay longer and help his fellow soldiers. With that kind of experience behind him, it came as no surprise to his fellow police officers that his true dedication was to his family and his faith. He was the proud father of a three-year-old son, Milton, and two daughters Tanya, three, and Michelle, six. In more than six years of service in the department, he had spent much of his time playing ball with the kids in the neighborhood and talking with them. In addition to his love of children, he played the violin for his church choir.

In a typical Baltimore neighborhood, children play long after dark, and summer vacation brings many people outside to escape the heat inside their houses. Around 9:30 P.M. on the night of August 15, 1974, as Officer Spell patrolled among the many residents of the 1600 block of North Bradford, he spotted what he believed to be a drunk driver. He stopped the motorist in the block and called for backup, not knowing that Avon Mason Simmons, sitting in the driver's seat of what was a stolen car, had a pistol ready. Milton Spell had stopped the car to keep the suspected drunk from killing anyone unfortunate enough to step into his way.

Officer Spell went to the driver's side and asked to see a license and registration. He had no chance to pull his own pistol in self-defense before Simmons unleashed two shots. The first bullet pierced Milton's heart, the second lodged in his abdomen. Officer Louis Michelberger, only seconds away, heard the shots and found his fellow officer in the middle of a crowd, lying on his back and bleeding from the two wounds. He performed CPR until an ambulance arrived from the Johns Hopkins Hospital, but the best efforts of all who worked to save Milton's life were in vain. The bullet that pierced his heart caused irreparable damage. After only twenty-one minutes on the operating table, Milton Spell died. Doctors and police officials made sure that a Roman Catholic priest was on hand to administer the sacrament of Last Rites in his final moments.

Officer Spell's killer was located only with the efforts of the city's best homicide detectives, who found themselves up against a community that preferred to keep silent rather than help a man who had cared so much about serving others. Although it was difficult to find someone who would volunteer information about the suspected killer, there was no shortage of people to tell of the officer's love of community. He was "just a nice dude, he used to play a lot with the kids in the neighborhood," a local resident recalled.

Patrolman Martin J. Greiner

December 10, 1974, Northern District
2 years and 6 months of service

Several citizens in the Remington neighborhood called for help when they heard gunshots near the intersection of 27th Street and Huntingdon Avenue on November 30, 1974, shortly after two in the morning. In Baltimore, officers respond to several calls for the discharging of firearms during a regular week's work and consider them almost routine. Even though frequent and often unfounded, no officer approaches this type of call without exercising caution. Such was the case when Officer Martin Greiner arrived on scene and found four people standing on the corner.

He stepped from his patrol car and focused on the group, who stared back at him. Before Greiner could act, William E. Teves III separated himself from the others, raised his pistol, and fired several times. One shot struck Greiner in the stomach, dropping him to the ground. As Teves fled the scene, Greiner clawed his way back to the patrol car and broadcast a description of his assailant. Officers and medics rushed to his side and got him to Union Memorial Hospital, where he was taken into surgery. Just a few blocks away, backup officers spotted Teves running. In the 2600 block of Mace Street officers chased the armed man on foot and in a coordinated effort cornered Teves in the 2600 block of North Charles Street. Teves resisted and was injured during the fight.

As Greiner lay in his hospital bed, his fellow officers led Teves into the room so the wounded officer could identify him. When the positive identification was made, Teves lunged at Greiner. Shortly afterward, police took Teves to Mercy Hospital for treatment of the injuries he sustained during the arrest. Mercy admitted the violent criminal and put him in a room where Officers John Burns and John Provenza guarded him. Even though the suspect was unarmed, the two officers kept a careful vigil, Provenza outside the room to watch for any friends and family of the suspect who might try to free him, and Burns inside to keep him from attempting an escape.

Teves tried to distract Burns by asking for help using the restroom. When Burns obliged, Teves reached for Burns's weapon. The move caught Burns by surprise, and though he struggled for the gun he soon lost control. Teves was able to shoot Burns twice before Provenza heard the sounds of the struggle and entered the room. Provenza leveled his revolver and shot Teves in the abdomen, ending the fight. Soon after the shooting of Greiner and Burns, it was discovered that Teves was suspected of shooting Officer James Harris in 1972. Because of his new gunshot wound, Teves was admitted to the hospital for long-term care and kept under armed guard.

Ten days later, on December 10, 1974, Officer Martin Greiner died of infection caused by a bullet lodged in his spine. Despite the best efforts of doctors, and numerous antibiotics, the infection spread from his spine to his brain, resulting in death. Soon after, Teves was charged with murder. Officer Martin Greiner was the fourth officer killed in the line of duty in 1974, the second worst year in the department's history after 1965, and a number not to be equaled until 2000. The tragically high number of officers killed in 1974 led the city to equip all of its police with bullet-proof vests. Since then, the vest has been credited with saving many lives nationwide.

Officer Greiner was only twenty-five years old at the time of his death and was survived by his mother Clara and his sister Maryann. As news of Martin's death spread, the department fell into the all too familiar routine of placing mourning bands over badges and driving with headlights on to signify a department in mourning.

PATROLMAN EDWARD S. SHERMAN

September 13, 1975, Southwestern District
5 years of service

Early on the morning of September 13, 1975, Officer Edward Sherman parked his car behind the Edgewood Elementary School. He was taking a break from a hard tour of duty on the midnight shift in the Southwestern District. He backed his car against a curb and chain-link fence to guard against anyone approaching from behind. He was perhaps unaware that a thick, deep undergrowth of weeds covered the exhaust pipes of his patrol car.

He began to feel drowsy as he relaxed, but he was not concerned; after all, the midnight shift has often had that effect. He also did not know that a piece of rubber was missing from the trunk lining of his car, allowing carbon monoxide to creep into the passenger compartment. An unwitting victim of carbon monoxide poisoning rarely has a chance to defeat its deadly effects. In all likelihood, Officer Sherman thought he was just tired as he nodded off. Slowly, the carbon monoxide replaced the oxygen in his body, depriving him of his life. He died peacefully.

When his fellow officers did not hear from him after a while, they tried to locate him. The closer they came to the end of the shift, the harder they looked. It was unlike Officer Sherman to go too long without meeting with someone during the boring hours of the midnight shift. His friends, Officers Martin and Gooden, found him at ten minutes after seven. They beat on the window in an effort to wake him as the engine continued to run. Fearing the worst, they smashed the patrol car's window. Martin pulled him from the car and began CPR, but it was too late. All their efforts were in vain. On Wednesday, September 17, 1975, Officer Edward Sherman, a five-year veteran was laid to rest, the victim of tragic circumstance.

Patrolman Timothy B. Ridnour

October 27, 1975, Southwestern District
11 months of service

Officers Timothy Ridnour and Bernard Harper responded to a call for a mentally deranged man running naked through his neighborhood. In the 4400 block of Old Frederick Road they found the man acting erratically, running from one area to another, and placing Christmas decorations on a tree growing in the apartment complex. Confounded by his strange behavior, the officers approached him cautiously. The man sprinted past them and sat in the passenger side of their patrol car. Their gentle, non-confrontational approach did not ease the situation. Faced with someone who did not understand reason, their frustrations were compounded by the man's refusal to communicate. Once again they approached him, and once again he sprinted away.

Officer Harper had summoned backup and steadily attempted to calm the man by explaining that they were there to help and not hurt him. When the officers were finally able to close the distance, he assumed a defensive boxer-style stance, and pointed at the revolver in Officer Ridnour's holster, hinting at what was about to follow. Ridnour reached down to check his pistol and the safety strap. Seconds later the unthinkable happened. The suspect attacked Ridnour and wrestled him to the ground. Officer Harper joined the fight and used all his strength to separate the two. Ridnour attempted to create a margin of safety by jumping a hedge. He failed to clear it and fell to the ground with the mentally deranged man jumping on top of him. Before Harper could help his partner, the suspect had successfully ripped the service revolver from Ridnour's holster and stood above him as he lay on the ground. With no trace of remorse, he fired five shots into Officer Ridnour's head, just as the backup units arrived.

Officer Harper realized he needed more firepower and retrieved the shotgun from the trunk of his car. As Ridnour lay on the ground, barely alive, the suspect used his spare ammunition to reload. He then stood up to engage the officers again. A blast from Officer Harper's shotgun killed him. Officer Ridnour made it to Saint Agnes Hospital, where the medical staff worked to save his life. Sadly, he was pronounced dead at 5:06 P.M. on October 27, 1975. A civilian who had attempted to help the officers had also been shot but survived the incident.

In loving memory of my Jimmy

God Bless,
Angie Halcomb

PATROLMAN JIMMIE D. HALCOMB

April 16, 1976, Western District
7 years of service

Angie Halcomb stood alone at the podium. More than twenty-five years after her husband's life had been stolen, she was there to dedicate a memorial at the corner of Fayette and President Streets. The unseasonably warm sun offered a perfect day, while she gazed skyward looking for courage and words to speak. City leaders, past and present police commissioners, honor guards, respected members of the community, husbands, wives, brothers, sisters, nieces, nephews, all shared her grief at the loss of a loved one. Yet she stood alone. After glancing to her left and seeing the sea of dress blue uniforms, she began to speak. She spoke of the love for her husband, the hard work that had brought this day together, and the need to never forget. On All Saints Day of 2003, she and those who worked diligently with her dedicated a place of remembrance for all to share.

On April 16, 1976, Officer Jimmie Halcomb had responded to a community's desperate call for help. Sniper fire rained down on the 1300 block of West Lombard Street. Several districts, including the Southern, Southwestern, Western and the Tactical Section sent officers in an attempt to bring the situation under control. Thirty-one-year-old Jimmie Halcomb of the Western District Operations Unit was among the first to arrive. He took cover behind his car and began to work with other officers on a plan to stop the madman. As he crouched behind his car, the sniper fired a round that smashed through the sheet metal and struck him. Moments later, Jimmie was dead.

The sniper continued firing, wounding Officer James Brennan as the patrolman took a position of advantage behind a van on Carey Street and striking Officer Roland Miller in his left arm. Officers Splain, Mencken, and Kennel of the Southern District worked their way to the rear of the suspect's rowhouse and were all hit with shotgun blasts. After nearly forty-five minutes, the suspect called the Communications Division and told of his plans to surrender. When he was taken into custody, one of the department's worst days came to a close. Jimmie Halcomb was a loving husband and father who wanted to protect his loved ones most of all.

More than twenty-five years later, Angie Halcomb stood alone at a podium with only her husband's memory by her side.

Police Officer Edgar J. Rumpf

February 15, 1978, Central District
6 years and 11 months of service

Black smoke billowed out of the windows of a second floor apartment at 1526 Park Avenue. Officers in the area responded and called for the city fire department. Before those brave men and women could arrive, the officers went about the business of saving people's lives, going door-to-door and alerting residents in the apartment building. The fire got further and further out of control, until it had grown to a third alarm.

The chatter on the Central District radio was that of the officers checking on each other as the mission of lifesaving became increasingly more perilous. Eventually the retreat was sounded and one by one the officers made their way back to safety. The dispatcher conducted a roll call in order to make certain that all of the officers were out of the building. Then, from the officers' radios, came a sound that made all hearts sink. Officer Edgar Rumpf was stuck in an elevator unable to escape, beyond the reach of officers and firefighters.

The fire grew still more fierce, reaching six alarms by 2:30 P.M. Firefighters attempted to follow screens of water into the building in a vain attempt to reach Officer Rumpf. As they made their way deeper into the building, the rescuers became trapped themselves, surrounded by walls of fire. Eventually they were rescued, but the result was clear—any effort to reach Officer Rumpf would result in great loss of life. The fire reached nine alarms before it was brought under control. Like so many officers before him, Officer Edgar J. Rumpf sacrificed his life in the attempt to save others, and indeed, on that terrible afternoon many lives in an apartment building on Park Avenue were saved as the direct result of his selfless act.

Sergeant Robert J. Barlow

April 23, 1978, Tactical Section
19 years of service

One of the best things about being a Baltimore Police Officer is the chance to work Baltimore Orioles games. For years, the citizens of Charm City watched their favorite team from the seats of Memorial Stadium on East 33rd Street. Standing proudly between the quiet neighborhoods of the Northeast District and City College High School, it was home to the Baltimore Colts and the renowned

Johnny Unitas, and the place where the Baltimore Orioles had made history in the World Series. It has been the responsibility of the department to provide a secure and safe environment for sports fans to watch their teams. This is not to say that spectators are at risk of being victims of criminal activity, but there is always a need for police help finding lost children, answering medical emergencies, recovering lost items, and dealing with over-zealous fans who have had too much to drink.

For the most part, officers who work the games do so as an overtime shift. The Tactical Section, though, is usually detailed to these events to supplement the overtime force. This was the case on April 23, 1978. Sergeant Robert Barlow was detailed to supervise the officers who would perform traffic control before and after the game as well as those who monitored sections 37 through 41 within the stadium. Lt. Phillip Farace arrived at the stadium just before 11 A.M. on game day and found Sergeant Barlow already hard at work. To find the sergeant at work early was not unusual. He cared about the men and women he supervised and did his best to thoroughly prepare for each tour of duty. Lieutenant Farace, noticing that the sergeant was sweating and that he appeared pale, asked if anything was wrong. Sergeant Barlow had already kick-started all of the Tactical Section's motorcycles and had had significant trouble with one. He told Lieutenant Farace that he needed a moment to catch his breath and that he would be all right.

On this late April day, Sergeant Barlow was going to be called on time and time again to assist his fellow officers and citizens needing help. During the opening ceremonies, Bessie Kaufman suffered a stroke. Sergeant Barlow and the medical team, led by Firefighters Lloyd Marcus and John Trawinski, sprinted up the steep steps of Section 41 to the seventy-four-year-old woman. She was unable to walk and Sergeant Barlow lifted her with the help of a medic and carried her to the stretcher. The medical personnel took Ms. Kaufman to the aid station, and Sergeant Barlow went back to work. An hour and a half later, the call for a medical emergency went out again.

Carol Ward found Sergeant Barlow and asked for his assistance. She could not find where her family was seated, and Sergeant Barlow did his best to help her. After climbing the steps of several sections, Mrs. Ward and Sergeant Barlow came upon her family. Mrs. Ward thanked Sergeant Barlow for his help only to run back to him with a real emergency. Her mother, Winifred, had lost consciousness. Once again, Sergeant Barlow sprinted into the stands with the medical team to provide much needed aid. They had to carry the unconscious woman over several seats to the stretcher. It was later determined that Winifred had suffered a heart attack and that Sergeant Barlow's actions had helped save her life. Several officers approached the sergeant after these stressful events and noticed that he was pale and sweating heavily. He brushed off their comments, citing his age and telling them that he was "getting too old for this stuff." Moments later, he went to the aid of an eighty-four-year-old man who was feeling faint. Because there was no medical team available, Sergeant Barlow and the usher supervisor pulled the stretcher five sections to the medical aid station.

At 6:30 P.M. Sergeant Barlow was relieved of duty and went home. Just before he left, Sgt. Norman Parker pulled him aside and asked if he felt all right and if he needed help. He replied, "I am extremely tired and am going right home and just relax." He told Sergeant Parker he was "getting too old for this running up and down these ramps and you are going to have to take over the up and down assignments." Then he went home to spend the evening with his wife Willa and daughters Catherine and Barbara. Robert Barlow, who loved spending time with his family, sat on his living room couch and waited for dinner. Soon after, Willa heard her daughters scream, "Daddy! Daddy! What's the matter?" She rushed in to find her husband slumped over, holding his chest, gasping for breath and unable to speak.

An ambulance took him to Union Memorial Hospital, where at 8:25 P.M. Robert Barlow was pronounced dead of a heart attack. After a thorough investigation, the Board of Trustees of the Fire and Police Retirement System determined that Sergeant Barlow's death was the result of his actions in the line of duty. That decision provided a measure of stability and security for those he cared for most, his wife and daughters.

Police Officer Nelson F. Bell, Jr.

October 27, 1978, Tactical Section – K9 Unit, 4 years and 10 months of service

Harvey Zuckerman, a twenty-two-year-old from Frostburg, was a volatile and extremely disturbed man. On October 22, 1978, he packed his luggage with various weapons and made his way to the Trailways Bus Station in the 200 block of West Fayette Street. At half past three in the afternoon, he arrived at the depot, approached the ticket window, and attempted to cash a bank draft for $455.25. The ticket agent, Mrs. Pluma Lee, politely declined his attempt to cash the note, and he walked away. For the next several hours, Mr. Zuckerman attracted the attention of all those who did business inside the station, for he was dressed in a cowboy hat and boots and spent long hours standing completely still, pretending to be a statue. When he did break his stance he moved about the area making mock karate movements and swinging his hat in circles.

Travelers and passersby took note of his strange behavior but continued on their way. As the afternoon wore on toward evening,

Zuckerman's behavior took on a whole new character. He opened his luggage and began to lay out weapons for all to see. In the rear alley where the buses loaded, he carefully placed his ax, compound bow and arrow, and a .30-.30 rifle with several boxes of ammunition on a waist-high retaining wall. This new threat brought immediate attention, and police quickly made their way to the scene. A standoff ensued, as Officers took positions of tactical advantage, isolating the armed man and protecting the citizens who sought their own cover. Among those responding to the scene was K9 Officer Nelson Bell.

Bell took a position behind a massive bus, out of the direct line of fire, while his fellow officers demanded that Zuckerman drop the compound bow. But there would be no reasoning with the deranged man. The officers' shouts grew louder until the tension reached the breaking point. Zuckerman drew an arrow back and began to run toward one officer with the scream of a warrior. Several officers opened up. The firefight was one-sided and ended very quickly. After only six or seven steps, and twenty-five shots fired by the police, the bow and arrow fell from Zuckerman's hands, and he collapsed.

Stopping the madman brought a sense of relief to everyone at the scene, but among police officers relief turned to horror as they noticed Officer Bell slumped over and bleeding profusely. Somehow, a bullet from one of their guns had ricocheted and struck him in the neck. They rushed Bell to University Hospital's Institute for Emergency Medical Services, where doctors discovered that after the bullet struck Officer Bell it had broken into two pieces. One fragment had traveled deep into his brain, causing the fatal damage. For six days Nelson hung onto life in his hospital bed with friends and family by his side. On October 27, 1978, at five minutes past eleven, Officer Nelson Bell died. Nelson was the proud father of three children. Twelve hours before the shooting on that fateful day, he and his wife Karin, along with his sons Randy and Timothy, had attended the christening of his three-week-old daughter Colleen.

Police Officer William D. Albers

August 19, 1979, Eastern District
11 years of service

Throughout their storied history, the doctors of the Johns Hopkins Hospital have helped save the lives of many Baltimore residents with their expertise and skill. In addition to treating physical injuries and illnesses, Johns Hopkins has also made great efforts to solve psychiatric problems.

Early on the morning of July 30, 1979, Willie Shaw voluntarily checked himself into the emergency room in search of psychiatric care. Situated in the center of one of the city's most violent neighborhoods, Hopkins has routinely hired police officers to supplement their own security forces. That same morning, Officer William Albers was on duty, safeguarding patients and employees in the hospital.

Shaw was agitated and in need of immediate help. Doctors made the decision to sedate him, and he was given medication to calm him. While the medicine was being administered, his wife and medical professionals worked to arrange permanent care in a "non-state" hospital. The sedative caused Shaw to sleep peacefully in a temporary psychiatric care room near the emergency room. When the time came to transfer him to the permanent care site, Officer Albers accompanied the doctor and nurse. At 10:15 A.M. Shaw was once again in an agitated state and difficult to control. The physician decided to inject another dose of the sedative. They left Shaw alone in the room, intending to give the medication time to work. Officer Albers was the last to leave.

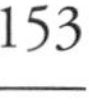

Albers paused at the doorway as the doctor and nurse continued on their way. When he tried to secure the door, Shaw attacked him. The entire gruesome scene unfolded on the monitor that nurses use to keep watch over their patients. Unaffected by the sedative, Shaw leaped to his feet and went straight for the officer's weapon, ripping it cleanly from the holster without warning. Albers reacted, turning and raising his right arm in an instinctive and vain attempt to stop the first bullet. That shot went through the officer's outstretched hand. Though wounded, Albers fought to get his gun back. As the men struggled for the weapon, Shaw repeatedly pulled the trigger. In seconds the gun was empty and both men fell to the floor. William had been shot five times in the arms, legs, and thighs. Shaw had been shot once in the chest.

The fight for the gun lasted but a few seconds, and as soon as the hospital staff came out of their places of protective cover, help arrived. Shaw's wound resulted in almost immediate death. Officer Albers made it into surgery, a marathon session that lasted for hours and required nearly fifty pints of blood. He emerged in critical condition, and over the next three weeks hopes for his recovery rose and fell. By the twentieth day, doctors felt that he was not going to recover and summoned his family. At one o'clock in the afternoon on August 19, 1979, William Albers died.

William was an eleven-year veteran of the department and had served as a turnkey in the Eastern District station house. He cared deeply for his family and worked at the hospital to provide for them. His wife Cynthia, daughters Susan and Cindy, son Scott, and stepsons John, David, James, and Donald were with him on his last day.

Police Officer Ronald Tracey

July 20, 1981, Western District
7 years and 4 months of service

A small crowd had gathered to watch Officer Tracey manage the aftermath of an automobile collision at the corner of Monroe and Baker Streets in the Western District just before midnight on July 20, 1981. It was a warm night, and citizens had gathered to watch tow trucks lift the damaged cars. But in that crowd was a man who quietly made his way toward the unsuspecting officer and, for no apparent reason, attacked him.

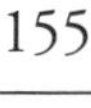

The deranged man jumped on Officer Tracey's back, and a mortal struggle began. Officers in the Western District heard a jumbled, frantic call for help over their radios. They could not make out clearly what was being said, nor could they figure out who was in trouble or where. For several minutes Tracey and his attacker wrestled as the citizens watched. No one offered assistance. A witness did call in to the Communications Center and reported the fight. The assailant snatched Tracey's weapon from his holster, and the two fought over the service revolver with all the strength they could muster until the suspect gained control of the weapon and fired a round into Tracey's stomach.

The citizens' call to communications did not produce help quickly enough. As officers began to respond to the scene, the suspect stood over their wounded comrade and fired a second shot into his head, killing him instantly. The crowd watched the murder. Not a person stepped forward to help, or even to prevent the escape of the murderer. In a violent district such as the Western, citizens rarely come forward to help one another, let alone a police officer in need, out of the pervasive, overriding fear of retaliation from the criminal element among them. Eventually, people began calling in anonymous tips about the identity and whereabouts of the ruthless animal who had callously taken the life of one of the city's finest protectors.

A massive manhunt began with a sense of unparalleled urgency. At five o'clock on the morning of July 21, 1981, officers located the murderer sleeping on the basement floor of a Northeast District home and arrested him. The reasons for his attack on Officer Tracey remain unknown. It was absolutely unexpected and a reminder that no matter the nature of the call, danger is always present.

The bond between officers is strong, and only grows stronger when one of their own loses his life in the line of duty, at the hands of citizens they are sworn to protect.

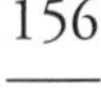

Detective Marcellus Ward

December 3, 1984, Narcotic Enforcement (Detailed to the Drug Enforcement Administration), 13 years of service

The last traces of sunlight had just faded on the afternoon of December 3, 1984. Detective Marcellus "Marty" Ward was on the third floor of a Southwest Baltimore rowhouse with one of the city's most dangerous drug dealers. Marty was a hugely successful undercover officer. In a matter of months he had managed to infiltrate a gang of men who trafficked in very large amounts of heroin. In the mid-1980s, Baltimore was in the grip of a drug epidemic that threatened to destroy inner-city neighborhoods. The signs and symptoms of a city in crisis demanded that the battle lines of the drug war be drawn in the streets.

Marty Ward accepted his role in this fight and took on the most dangerous of jobs. For an undercover officer, backup is always too far away. Success and safety depend on his or her ability to balance the need to think like a cop while acting like a thug. The conclusion of a long and dangerous investigation was only moments away as Marty sat on the couch in Lascell Simmons' apartment. The plan as drawn up by a team of city narcotics detectives and drug enforcement agents had gone well prior to the scheduled 5:45 P.M. raid. A separate squad of officers had already arrested one member of Simmons' gang at a nearby train station as he met undercover officers in a set-up.

Moments later, officers and agents crashed through the front door of the candy store at 1829 Frederick, and started up the stairs to Simmons' apartment. The commotion alerted the drug dealer, who prepared for a standoff by arming himself with a .357 caliber handgun. As the raiding party made its way up the stairs, all froze when they heard the sounds of a struggle from within the apartment. Suddenly, shots rang out from the third floor. One of Marty's best friends, Gary Childs, heard the gunfire and his heart sank. Marty had been shot four times, twice in the chest. He fell back onto the couch and could no longer offer any resistance. Simmons turned his attention to the men climbing the stairs and concentrated on keeping them at bay.

The officers now had a new mission—getting to their wounded comrade in time. Simmons refused to allow them to climb the stairs. In a deadpan voice he repeatedly demanded, "Uniformed police only." Gary Childs screamed for his friend. "Marty!" he yelled over and over again, throwing his badge and wallet onto the floor in front of Simmons in an effort to prove they were indeed officers of the law. Despite the obvious fact that Ward's wounds were serious and probably fatal (and doubtless fully aware of it), Simmons refused to allow any help to reach the man he had just shot. Eventually, Simmons threw his handgun and Marty's service weapon onto the hallway floor and allowed the officers to enter.

Gary rushed in and tried to save the life of a man he treasured as his closest friend by breathing life into Marty's body. He was still holding Marty in his arms when his friend died, in that southwest neighborhood above a candy store.

Marty Ward was more than just a good cop. When people gathered to remember him, they remembered man who cared deeply about others. Titles did not mean much to him. He treated those around him with respect and compassion, no matter their social status. When he dealt with informants and those addicted to drugs, he saw people who still deserved to be treated humanely. Regardless of the crime a person committed, Marty would never be disrespectful or try to humiliate him. "When he had to be tough, he was tough, but he always had compassion for people, always," Gary said. Marty's identity was not defined by the job he held; he was known for being what all people desire to be, a great person.

Police Officer Richard J. Lear

October 8, 1985, Northern District
31 years and 8 months of service

For most of his thirty-one years of service, Officer Richard "Richey" Lear walked a foot beat. His fellow officers and the citizens who knew him considered him an "old-time cop," and in the Hampden and Remington communities of Northern Baltimore he knew everyone and everyone knew him. He treasured his job and took the best care of those he was assigned to protect. At the age of sixty-one, he had seen the changes in policing brought about by radios, motorized patrols, and the development of the 911 system. His career spanned an era that defined policing from its roots to the modernization of law enforcement. To be in his shoes, was to have had a front seat to history in the making.

On the evening of October 8, 1985, Officer Lear was doing what he loved most, walking his beat, when an alarm sounded in the 5400 block of York Road. Lear walked over from his post to back up the officer assigned to the call. At fifteen minutes past eleven in the evening, he crossed one of the busiest sections of York Road in the city, just as a thirty-year-old drunk driver, Ramin Navai, was speeding south. Navai was on his way to a bar he owned on Greenmount Avenue called the "Dugout Tavern." Onlookers watched as Navai's dull white Pontiac Trans Am struck Lear and threw him seventy-five feet through the air. Navai did not stop.

Half an hour later, Richey Lear was pronounced dead in the emergency room of Sinai Hospital. Eventually Baltimore County Police arrested Navai at the intersection of York and Timonium Roads. Not only was he fleeing from the death he had caused, he had outstanding warrants for bad checks and driving on a suspended license. Because of the efficient communication and cooperation between the city and county police departments, Navai would now face charges of manslaughter, driving while intoxicated, and speeding.

Newspaper articles describing Richey Lear's untimely death were peppered with examples of his generosity and closeness to the members of the communities he patrolled. Ralph Baker, a retired city officer who was the chief of security at the Rotunda on West 40th Street, was quoted a few days after the incident as saying that Lear would "dig in his own pocket and take out $5 or $10" to help someone in need buy food. On a chilly October day, Richard Lear was laid to rest. Since 1945 he had spent his life, unmarried, living with and caring for his eighty-three-year-old mother. She was too ill to attend the funeral, so after his flag-draped coffin was carried from the church to the hearse, the procession drove by his house on South Charles Street so his mother could watch it pass.

Almost twenty years after his death, an initiative called "All Out" had many officers walking foot posts throughout the city. As the day wore on, conversations of these officers, mostly detectives, turned to the days when they had first walked beats. While they stood on the corner of Cottage and Oswego Avenues in a Northwest Baltimore neighborhood, Detectives Wayne Sponsky and Debbie Fox reminisced about Richey Lear. They talked about the days when they had first patrolled the streets of the Northern District and remembered how officers like Lear were respected and loved by their communities. A short distance away, Officer Siegfried "Ziggy" Weber, a man who had had the opportunity to work with Richey, went about his business at the Northern District Station House. Weber, an officer since 1969, remembered his first years walking a foot beat and how Richey Lear used to tease him and the other rookies. "He was a quiet guy that cared about the people in the neighborhood. He wasn't happy unless he was walking his beat," Weber recalled.

Police Officer Vincent J. Adolfo

November 18, 1985, Eastern District
3 years and 6 months of service

Most of the officers in the roll call room of the Eastern District could not control their emotions. Some sobbed openly while others wore the pain of loss on their tight-lipped faces. Less than twenty-four hours before, they had sat side by side with a young man who loved his job and loved the people with whom he worked. More than just the typical wide-eyed rookie, Officer Vinnie Adolfo spent his first three years of policing in a violent, distressed neighborhood, a place that would turn the hearts of lesser people to steel, without losing his resolve or faith in a city he lived in and loved. Just before his transfer request would take effect and send him to police the neighborhood in which he had grown up, Vinnie listened to the shift commander read out the reports of recent crimes and went back to work. Only a few hours later, Vincent J. Adolfo would die in the neighborhood in the shadow of the Johns Hopkins Hospital.

Vinnie had a unique ability to make quality arrests and took special delight in helping senior citizens and children. Early in the evening of November 18, 1985, he keyed up his radio and called in the tag of a Cadillac traveling eastbound on Biddle Street. Moments later he was coordinating an effort to stop the Cadillac, which turned out to have been recently stolen, near the intersection of Biddle and Broadway. With other officers close by, Officer Adolfo turned on his lights and siren to stop the car. There were four people in the Cadillac, but only the driver tried to run from the scene. Flint Gregory Hunt ran into the 1200 block of Iron Alley with Vinnie just steps behind him. The backup officer held the three passengers at gunpoint while his partner chased Hunt. Vinnie caught the car thief quickly and tried to handcuff him as the wanted man held onto a pole. Hunt used his weight and lunged backward, forcing Adolfo to take several steps away to regain his balance. Hunt had a large caliber pistol in his waistband that Vinnie had not yet removed.

Hunt drew the pistol, and fired point blank into the officer's bullet-resistant vest. The handgun's power and close range were too much for the departmentally issued vest, and Vinnie fell to the ground with a bullet lodged in his heart. Hunt stood over him and fired another round into the mortally wounded officer's back. The gun's report reached the back-up officers arresting the three other suspects less than a block away. By the time help reached him, Vinnie lay with his head propped against a brick wall, bleeding from two wounds. They tried desperately to save their young friend's life. CPR was immediate and the Johns Hopkins Hospital was only seven blocks away, but though Vinnie was on the operating table in minutes with one of the hospital's best heart surgeons, he was pronounced dead less than half an hour after first spotting the stolen Cadillac.

There was a special urgency in finding Flint Gregory Hunt so he could be brought to justice, but there were also pleas from Sgt. Richard Price, Vinnie's supervisor. "Please, if you see the rotten bastard out there, do it by the book." Originally, detectives believed that Hunt was still in the city, and the tactical teams crashed through several doors in an effort to locate him. In fact, Hunt had stolen another car and gone to New Jersey to escape capture. The search widened to encompass nearly the entire East Coast, but Hunt had purchased a one-way bus ticket to San Francisco. When his travel plans were discovered, he was found and arrested in Tulsa, Oklahoma. Eventually, Flint Gregory Hunt was executed for his crimes less than a mile from where he had taken Vincent Adolfo's life.

Twenty-five-year-old Vincent Adolfo was a beloved member of a large Catholic family who turned to each other and to his young widow, Karen, for solace after his death. But a larger family would come to the side of his immediate family to help with the healing that would never be complete. He was fondly remembered as always being professional and demanding the best from himself and those around him. Lt. Tom Keavney addressed the assembled officers when they returned to work the next day. Vinnie Adolfo "always had a smile . . . [he] would not like us to go out there tonight and be anything more than good cops you have been." Almost twenty years later, Karen Adolfo remembered her young husband as she stood next to her daughter and her fellow members of the Fraternal Order of Police Memorial Fund Committee and dedicated the loving memorial to our fallen officers now standing at the corner of Fayette and President Streets.

Police Officer Richard T. Miller

July 21, 1986, Traffic Division
32 years of service

Richard Miller was convinced that the Baltimore Orioles were going to the World Series in 1986. In fact, he had postponed his expected retirement in order to work through the season and enjoy his assignment to the Traffic Division, a unit assigned to every game to direct motorists around the stadium. Memorial Stadium on 33rd Street long had served as the home to the National Football League's Colts, recently moved to Indianapolis, and baseball's American League Orioles, but was dedicated as a memorial to those who had sacrificed their lives in World War II. The football-shaped structure was the pride and joy of the northeastern neighborhood, but Memorial Stadium offered police several unique challenges in ensuring the safety of the thousands of fans as they entered and left.

On June 12, 1986, Officer Miller was standing with two of his fellow officers making sure that no traffic moved westbound on 33rd Street. For whatever reason, Leonard P. Cirincione steered his 1977 Toyota pickup truck toward the officers. When Richard saw the truck coming he stepped out to flag down the motorist and turn him around. Cirincione showed no signs of slowing. Two other officers joined Richard in his effort to stop the speeding truck. It was immediately apparent to the three men that the truck was not going to obey their commands to stop.

What started as an effort to stop a vehicle traveling in the wrong direction soon became a desperate attempt to save themselves from the two-thousand-pound truck bearing down on them. Cirincione was steering directly toward the officers despite the largely open roadway available to him. Although he ran and dove to get out of the way, Officer Miller was hit squarely by the crazed motorist. His fellow officers narrowly escaped harm. Medics were on site and able to transport Richard to University of Maryland's Shock Trauma Center immediately. His injuries were severe.

In an attempt to stop infection and save Richard's life, doctors amputated one of his legs. For nearly a month and a half he lay in bed fighting for his life. Doctors operated several times to repair the damage, but though their efforts were valiant, death was inevitable. On July 21, 1986, at 3:05 A.M., Officer Miller died in his hospital bed. At the time of his death, Richard was fifty-five years old and survived by his wife Elizabeth, son Richard Jr., and daughter Patricia.

Police Officer Robert Alexander

September 20, 1986, Southwestern District
9 months of service

The two rookies stood on a corner and talked about whatever rookies talk about. Officer Robert Alexander and Officer Robert Anderson treasured working together because the older officers routinely ignored rookies. They depended on one another to work through situations on the street and learn together. The early morning of September 20, 1986, was no different. A routine traffic accident call for service at the corner of Frederick and Boswell Avenues demanded that Officer Alexander respond to help citizens in need. They told each other that they would continue their talk later, and Officer Alexander pulled away.

The accident involved a citizen who had stopped for a red light when another vehicle struck his truck from behind. Officer Alexander positioned his patrol car in such a way that it provided a margin of safety for himself and the citizens. He then activated his overhead strobes and takedown lights, illuminating the area and announcing his presence to other motorists. Without warning, a speeding Nissan pickup truck screamed around the corner and headed straight toward the accident scene.

The driver of the truck was drunk and the vehicle out of control as it bore down on Officer Alexander and those he was helping. Alexander did not hesitate. Placing himself in the direct line of danger, his very last act was to push the citizens out of the path of the oncoming truck, saving their lives. Too late to save himself, Officer

Alexander, was crushed beneath the truck as it flipped over on top of him. When the wreckage came to rest, both citizens whose lives he had saved and passersby, including off-duty officer John Parrott, rushed to his aid.

Because of his earlier request to care for those involved in the initial accident, an ambulance was only seconds away. All of these people came to rescue the rescuer but were too late. Officer Alexander died at the scene. Fellow police who knew him, knew that he cared about serving the city of Baltimore and that his selfless act was just the type of genuine thing that he would do.

Police Officer William J. Martin

October 10, 1989, Central District
10 years of service

For the third time in one night, Officers Herman Brooks and William "Billy" Martin made their way to a highrise in the the 1500 block of Pennsylvania Avenue and a housing project known for violence, to handle a citizen's complaint of drug dealing. Both had had many years of experience and had worked well together. In an effort to arrest the criminals who terrorized the people of this neighborhood, they had agreed to split up. Officer Brooks went to the rear of the location to catch anyone who would run from them, while Billy went inside and up to the second floor.

The presence of Officer Martin in a stairwell landing surprised a young man who was sitting there. Shawn Woodson, a violent drug dealer, was armed with a .38 caliber Colt Super 8 and drew it as

Officer Martin climbed the stairs. For no other reason than that he was a police officer, William Martin was shot twice in the head and once in the shoulder. His assailant made an attempt to escape by running to the lower level and out a rear door. The gunfire alerted Officer Brooks, who ran toward the sound.

As the shooter made his way down the stairs, Brooks met him. Again, there was gunfire, but this time Brooks had the advantage of surprise. Brooks drew his service revolver and got off several rounds, but in the gun battle he also received two bullets in the chest and a wound in the left hand. A veteran of the Baltimore and Philadelphia Police Departments, Herman Brooks had been through similar confrontations, and he was prepared—he was wearing a bulletproof vest. The urgent call for backup and a medic reached Officer Robin Johnson. Because Woodson had been shot in the hip, Officer Johnson soon located and arrested the gunman. An investigation immediately following the incident resulted in the arrest of Woodson's partner in crime, Tavon Hall.

Though Billy's friends worked feverishly to get him to a hospital, they could not save his life. Everyone loved Billy, but the bond he had with Herman Brooks was forged by the fact that they had trusted each other even in the most dangerous situations.

Billy's wife, Kim, and sons Patrick and William Jr., felt the love of an extended police family after his death. Thousands of officers from many other departments and several states attended his funeral at St. Mary Star of the Sea Church.

Police Officer Ira N. Weiner

September 21, 1992, Western District
4 years of service

The woman leaned out of her second floor bedroom window at 1929 West Mulberry and looked to Officer Ira Weiner for help. The early September morning was warm enough for most officers to wear their short-sleeve uniform shirts. It was 8:30 A.M. as Ira stood on the sidewalk, and this was his first call of the day. He listened to the frantic woman, trying to find out the nature of the trouble inside. Her nephew, Lewis Thomas Jr., was high on cocaine and had been thrashing about for most of the night. His crazy behavior had grown worse as the night turned to day. Now he had armed himself with an ice pick and was holding his aunt and her seven small children hostage in their house. Ira stood alone as the distant sirens of his backup units drew closer. The woman tossed the keys to her front door to him so he could gain entry. The radio mike crackled in his ear to wait for backup—but the children needed help now.

Officer Weiner was a smart and seasoned cop. His maturity and ability were well beyond his four years of law enforcement experience, but that's the way it is for the proud officers of the Western District. In an environment that demanded performance, Officer Weiner thrived. All Baltimore City officers learn quickly, but for those assigned to the Western, the learning curve is steeper and more demanding in this historically violent part of town. Ira cared deeply for children, so he decided to open the door and protect those who could not protect themselves. Ira turned on his flashlight, tucked it beneath his left arm, and withdrew his pistol. Next door on the front porch, Donald Pettiford watched as Officer Weiner entered the house. In a matter of moments, Pettiford heard the sounds of a violent struggle ending with gunshots.

When Ira made his way into the house, he saw Thomas standing in the dark with the ice pick in his hand. "What's the matter, buddy?" Ira said. "I want to die," Thomas replied, and then he attacked. The enraged man landed blow after blow with his ice pick forcing Ira to the floor. Injured and no longer able to resist, Weiner was helpless to stop Thomas from picking up his weapon and firing point blank into his head.

Officer Terry Hendrickson heard shots fired as he closed in on the house. He pulled his semi-automatic pistol and began trading shots with Thomas. Sgt. Jerry DeManns arrived with a shotgun, took a position of advantage over Hendrickson's shoulder, and fired a shot. With the boom of the shotgun still echoing in their ears, the two men advanced into the house with DeManns in the lead. Two more shotgun blasts struck the suspect as other officers rushed in to help. Thomas was still firing off rounds when DeManns' shotgun jammed. Four other officers opened up and hit Thomas with sixteen additional shots, killing him. An ambulance arrived and carried Ira Weiner, fatally injured, to the Maryland Shock Trauma Center. Ira was put on life support with little chance of survival. With Ira near death, his family gave permission for doctors to retrieve vital organs to be used for transplant, giving life to those in need.

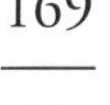

Ira was very special to many people and his death was crushing. Less than twenty-four hours before Ira was shot, a Southeastern District officer had also been shot in the head with his own weapon. Officer James E. Young Jr. had been working on a drug complaint that required him to go into the dangerous high rise known as Flag House Courts. He and his partner had split up and were making their way through the dark and run-down apartment building, not expecting the violence that followed. Three men, Sean Little, Kevin Green, and Vernon Silver, wrestled Young to the ground and took his weapon. These two outbursts of violence against police tested the mettle of the entire department and law-abiding community.

Officers demanded justice, Mayor Kurt L. Schmoke demanded the death penalty, and families tried to focus on their loved ones. In the following days, smiles emerged through tears as those who knew and loved Ira Weiner remembered all of the good that had surrounded a strong and quiet young man. Misting eyes and shaking voices recalled how Ira loved to play pool. "If anyone could trash talk and back it up on the pool table, Ira could," Terry Hendrickson recalled. It was not uncommon to find Ira playing pool at four or five o'clock in the morning after he had worked the four-to-midnight shift. On the billiards table in the station house, Ira welcomed all comers.

In a ceremony that combined the tradition of an Inspector's Funeral with the solemnity of a traditional Jewish ceremony, those in attendance heard the drone of bagpipes mingling with mourners' chanting of the Kaddish, the Jewish prayer for the dead. Rabbi Donald Berlin spoke highly of Ira Weiner and called for togetherness to help ease the grief. "This is a day when we need to join hands; black and white, Jew and Christian. This young man gave his life in the name of the law," he said. "I consider him a 'tsadic,' a saintly person, because of the service that he and all the other police are doing for us," said a civilian in attendance. His brothers and sisters in uniform made a promise to never let go of the memory of their fallen friend; as a daily reminder they mounted Ira's pool cue in the roll call room of the Western District.

Police Officer Herman A. Jones, Sr.

May 26, 1993, Central District
23 years of service

No one can ever doubt Herman Jones's love for Baltimore. His pride and loyalty in what he knew was a special place to live and work was undeniable. He grew up on the city's east side and spent his entire life learning and working in his hometown. Officer Herman Jones made a special connection to the people of the neighborhoods in which he served, because he understood the importance of partnerships. He saw himself as more than the protector of the weak and needy; in the larger picture he was one member of an able team, a team working to safeguard themselves from the few around them who had chosed the criminal life.

His love for Baltimore began in his early years when he played stickball in the alley behind his home on Wolfe Street with his closest friends. For a child, sports were a way to pass the time on lazy summer days. His passion for sports and his natural talent led to an outstanding high school career as a receiver on the City College's Maryland Scholastic Association football team. That team is well-known throughout the state as perennially one of the best, and to be recognized for his ability was a high honor. As he grew older, he did more than simply reminisce about his athletic days—he continued to show his pride by supporting his alma mater. His respect for tradition was what drove him to always attend the long-standing annual football game between City College and its equally famous rival, Baltimore Polytechnic Institute, or Poly.

His love for neighborhood, family, and Baltimore led directly to his desire to serve the city as a police officer. He had an innate ability to relate to people that many officers work many years to establish, and some never do. Early on the morning of May 26, 1993, Officer Jones put on a light windbreaker over his uniform shirt and left the Central District after working the four-to-midnight shift. He wore the jacket so he would not be recognized as an officer and become involved in trivial matters. On his way home he decided to stop, as he had many times before, at a local carry-out for a late night bite to eat. He entered the store and placed his order.

He had no way of knowing that three young men were watching and had decided to rob him. Two of the youths were inside the carry-out pretending to read a wall menu. The third was outside keeping an eye out for any on-duty police. It is most likely that the three boys had no idea that he was an officer.

The two inside the store seized the surprised officer and slammed him into a wall, then forced him down on the ground. The third boy entered and pointed a .38 caliber revolver at Jones. In an effort to distract his assailants, Herman threw whatever he had in his pockets out onto the floor. When they began to scramble after the valuables, Herman pulled his semi-automatic Glock pistol from his holster and began firing in self-defense.

He fired five shots, striking two of his attackers. They shot back, striking him twice. In a matter of seconds, the exchange of gunfire was over. Herman had focused his shots on Herbert Wilson, the seventeen-year-old boy with the revolver. He hit Wilson in the thigh and sixteen-year-old Derrick Broadway in the upper chest and shoulder. Clifton Price, seventeen, was not hit. But Jones was seriously wounded. The bullet that entered his left thigh had severed his femoral artery, a fatal injury. Herman slumped to the floor. The boys then stole his departmental handgun and ran from the scene. Responding officers got Herman to the Johns Hopkins Hospital immediately, but the damage to his femoral artery was too great for doctors to repair. Barely two hours after he was shot, Herman Jones was dead. Police followed a trail of blood from the scene to find Derrick Broadway, and the information they gained from him led to the arrest a few hours later of Price and Wilson at their homes.

Herman had touched the lives of many people in his fifty years of life, and when he is remembered, it is with pleasant memories. His friends reflect only momentarily on his brutal murder and instead tell stories of a funny, loving, and wonderful man. More than ten years later, his wife Linda is still doing what she knows her husband would have liked her to do, working side by side with others who have felt the same pain of loss. As a member of the Fraternal Order of Police Memorial Fund Committee, she has worked diligently to establish and oversee the construction of an important memorial honoring all Baltimore City Police Officers who have lost their lives in the line of duty. Her determination and straightforward style surely would have made Herman proud.

Police Officer Gerald M. Arminger

June 24, 1994, Southeastern District
21 years and 2 months of service

On June 22, 1994, two days after his forty-first birthday, Gerald "Mike" Arminger did what he did best—he worked the streets of the Southeastern District where he had started as a footman twenty-one years before. During his career he had witnessed the final transitions from foot posts to motorized patrol, and from call boxes to personal radios. Mike took pride in the role of a "beat cop" and rejoiced in the camaraderie of his squad. Even though his personnel jacket was stuffed with letters of commendation, bronze stars, unit citations, and other accolades, he chose to stay in patrol, a position many young officers work to leave behind as soon as they can.

Mike stayed in good physical shape because he knew the one constant when it comes to policing is that police officers age and criminals never do. For twenty-one years, he had chased eighteen-year-olds day after day. At the end of this particular shift, he sat in an office cubicle used by the patrol officers for administrative tasks, rocking back in his chair. He was talking to his friend, Officer Melvin Penn, and telling him about the latest foot chase he had had just two hours before. Penn was introducing Mike to a new friend, and they were getting along wonderfully. Just before 4 P.M., in the midst of a joyous gathering, he suffered a massive heart attack inside the District where he had spent his career. His friends started CPR immediately, but he went into convulsions and was taken to Francis Scott Key Hospital within minutes. Dr. Bessmon pronounced Mike, the beloved father of twins and husband of Melanie, dead in the emergency room, shortly after he arrived.

His family and friends were confused about his death. Here was a man who had appeared to be in good health, who had exhibited none of the common signs of stress and heart disease outside of occasional heartburn. At the request of his family and friends, the department made a full investigation to determine whether his death was line-of-duty related. The best doctors in the city came together and explored every detail. After thorough and complete research, the unanimous decision was reached that the stress of the foot chase on the day of his death caused the fatal attack. Officially, doctors ruled that if Mike had not been involved in that particular incident on that particular day, his heart attack never would have occurred.

Twelve years before he died, Mike had had a chance to leave the department and join the Maryland State Police. He had accepted a position in the 83rd Trooper Candidate Class and had written a letter of resignation on June 28, 1982. But Mike could not leave the city he loved. Less than two weeks later, he changed his mind. "I realized I made a mistake by resigning," he wrote in a departmental memo requesting his resignation be rescinded. He couldn't leave Baltimore. This city meant too much to him.

Mike was loved and admired by all who came in contact with him. His fellow officers knew about the numerous awards he received over the years, including being named Policeman of the Year, twice. His friends and family knew about his work with the Narcotics Task Force in the early eighties, resulting in thousands of arrests and seizures of hundreds of firearms. They also knew how he confronted the most dangerous criminals, armed with the most deadly weapons, and he never let his fellow officers down. Despite a chest full of medals, he was a humble man, who cared most about his fellow officers and neighbors. The greatest impact he made, however, was on a community that was safe, just because he went to work every day.

Lieutenant Owen E. Sweeney, Jr.

May 7, 1997, Northeastern District
28 years and 11 months of service

Eight hundred and fifteen days before he was going to retire, Lt. Owen E. Sweeney was sitting in the Northeastern District, laboring over tedious paperwork. Lieutenant Sweeney had the reputation of being someone who looked for the good in people and did his best to ensure the safety of the officers assigned to his shift. He was described by all who knew him well as a "cop's cop," and as Officer John Platt, a close friend of Sweeney's said, it was not beneath him, "because he wore a gold badge, to do police work with the rest of us."

Owen Sweeney's passion was working on the street with the officers on his watch. In the 5900 block of Bertram Avenue a call was dispatched for a family disturbance. Officers on scene discovered that Baron Michael Cherry had barricaded himself in a second floor bedroom. His wife reported that he was unarmed but very dangerous and in dire need of help. Lieutenant Sweeney walked into the house with Officer Platt to try to calm a volatile situation by establishing common ground with the troubled man. He spoke through a locked wooden door to a man on the edge. "We're here to help you, we're not here to hurt you," he said with the even tone for which he was known. Cherry did not answer and resisted Lieutenant Sweeney's attempts to communicate with him.

It soon became tragically clear that Cherry was not unarmed but had a shotgun. As Lieutenant Sweeney turned around to escape down the narrow stairway, he let Officer Platt go in front of him, his last act as a supervisor who prided himself on the safety of his officers. A shotgun blast ripped through the door and struck him in the back. He fell into the arms of Officer Platt who carried him out of the line of fire. Seconds afterward, officers were stunned to see Cherry walk out the front of his house, hands in the air, surrendering and apologizing at the same time.

Owen Sweeney died after three hours of surgery at the Maryland Shock Trauma Center. He was the first lieutenant to die while on his regular tour of duty, and the impact on the department was profound. The next day, a picture of a grief-stricken officer leaning on the hood of a patrol vehicle, crying, and in doing so expressing the sentiments of an entire police family, was on the front page of the local newspaper. Years later, his immediate family stood together with other members of the Fraternal Order of Police Memorial Committee as they dedicated a monument to his memory and to the many other officers who have sacrificed their lives in the service of Baltimore City, heroes in how they lived and served.

Police Officer Harold J. Carey

October 30, 1998, Central District
6 years of service

Officer Harold J. Carey was eating a quick breakfast at Howard and West 25th Streets, a diner where officers often gathered in the morning. The waitresses loved to see Carey in the morning because he always brought good-natured conversation and a warm smile. It was comical to see his huge six-foot one-inch, 250-pound frame jammed into the tiny booths inside the restaurant. On this particular morning he joked about a shoplifter who had been caught stealing Kool-Aid packets.

The food was always delicious, but this morning it had to be put aside to help a fellow officer involved in a tough struggle with a man in the 1900 block of North Charles Street, not quite six blocks away. He climbed into the wagon's passenger seat and his good friend, Officer Kevin Owens, got behind the wheel. They turned on their emergency lights and siren and headed south on Maryland Avenue.

Less than two blocks away from their fellow officer in need, they collided with another police vehicle responding to the same call. As they traveled south on Maryland Avenue, they had a green light at West 20th Street. Officer Owens had no chance to slow down and avoid the collision with the patrol car that roared out of 20th Street. The patrol car, intending a right turn onto Maryland Avenue, struck the van's passenger side front wheel sending it careening onto its side and into parked cars. The van finally came to rest on a parked car. Rescuers tried to cut the two officers free from the vehicle and render critical first aid, but it took nearly an hour to extract them from the wreckage. Officer Owens had a severe back injury from which he would eventually recover, but his friend had suffered fatal head and internal injuries.

On November 4, 1998, members of the Baltimore Police Department and many other neighboring agencies gathered to remember the life of one of the city's finest officers. It was a clear, cool afternoon as hundreds of police officers lined an expansive stretch of Edmondson Avenue. The flag-draped coffin was carried slowly down the steps of the church and walked passed the gauntlet of officers. The barked command to "Present Arms" sounded in the distance, and simultaneously all raised their right arms slowly to salute a fallen hero. In the stunning silence that followed, the radio broadcast another desperate cry for help. As the procession to take Officer Harold Carey to the cemetery started on its way, the engine of Flight Officer Barry Wood's helicopter failed, and it crashed to the city streets below. Officers started their brightly shined patrol cars and began to peel off the procession that would be hundreds of cars long, racing now to help yet another fatally injured officer.

Harold Carey was best known for his sense of humor. He valued laughter and never missed a chance to have a fun-filled conversation. Born and raised in Baltimore, he was most comfortable with his fellow officers and close friends around him. At work he concentrated on the children of the various neighborhoods he patrolled. Known as a gentle-giant, he also turned to his serious side and took care of business when it was time. He was a credit to the department and a mentor to other officers.

Flight Officer Barry W. Wood

November 4, 1998, Aviation Unit
27 years of service

All too often police officers face life-and-death situations alone. In a typical tour of duty, they run after dangerous criminals, confront armed people in dark, deserted alleys, and pray for fellow officers to arrive during those difficult moments. Police officers claim the Archangel Michael as their patron saint, and in Baltimore the sound of the beating blades of the helicopter they call Foxtrot represents the closest manifestation of that guardian angel, an unequalled source of comfort as it tracks criminals from the air.

When an officer needed a reliable protector, Flight Officer Barry Wood always did his utmost to provide that assistance. The beam of his powerful searchlight brought daylight to the darkest corners. His soothing voice, hallmark of the Foxtrot crew, allayed the fears of officers on foot. As Flight Officer Wood patrolled the skies above this city, he never took lightly the duty of watching over the neighborhoods below his aircraft, but he also knew that he and his crew had a still higher mission: to safeguard the city's protectors.

On November 4, 1998, as Baltimore mourned the loss of Officer Harold Carey and hundreds of highly polished police cars formed the long procession that would lay him to rest, Barry Wood took to the skies over Pratt Street to answer another call for help. Minutes later, trainees directing traffic listened in disbelief as their radios crackled: "Signal 13, Signal 13, 10-50 Red, Foxtrot has gone down." The

wail of sirens pierced the crisp morning air, and officers raced to help. What had begun as a routine call for assistance over Pratt Street ended with engine failure and catastrophe. In an attempt to land his aircraft with a maneuver called "autorotation," Barry tried to touch down in the B&O Railroad Museum's parking lot. Foxtrot's tail rotor apparently struck either a power line or a tree, which changed the attitude of the helicopter and drove it into the ground, killing him. Though severely injured, Barry's partner, Aerial Observer Mark Keller, survived the crash.

When the time came to lay Barry to rest, helicopters from many different agencies flew overhead in tribute as officers below saluted his flag-draped coffin. In the background, a speaker broadcast the dispatcher's last call for him: "KGA to Foxtrot . . . KGA to Foxtrot . . . Foxtrot is 10-5, not acknowledging."

The loss of Flight Officer Wood profoundly affected every officer in the department because the Foxtrot Fleet remained grounded during the extensive follow-up investigation, leaving Baltimore City's police officers to face dangers alone until a new fleet of aircraft arrived and resumed the role of guardian angels.

Police Officer Jamie A. Roussey

March 8, 2000, Western District
1 year and 1 month of service

On the night of March 8, 2000, the meaning of brotherhood once more became absolutely clear to everyone in the Baltimore Police Department. Many officers enjoy calling each other "brother" as a term of affection, but with Jamie, it was truly meant. "Jamie was raised by the Department," his father would say. As young as five years, Jamie would tell anyone who listened that he was going to be a police officer. So much of Jamie's family life revolved around the department it was as though Jamie had thousands of fathers, mothers, brothers, and sisters.

At the age of twenty-two, Jamie was the youngest member of the Roussey family to serve the citizens of Baltimore as a police officer. Along with his father, he also had a brother, an uncle, and a cousin on the force. Because of his upbringing, Jamie knew the importance of looking out for and watching over his fellow officers.

The call for help came from an officer in the middle of a foot chase through the violent Western District, where Jamie worked. Officer Roussey turned on his siren and emergency lights and went where he knew he needed to be. He headed north in the unit block of North Fulton Avenue, trying to balance listening to the desperate call on the radio with the demands of driving a patrol car through crowded city streets. As he entered the intersection of Fulton and Fayette Street, a Dodge Neon struck his patrol car broadside, forcing the driver's side into a utility pole. Officer Roussey died that night of internal injuries.

On the night of March 8, nearly 3,400 Baltimore Police Officers felt the crushing loss of another one of their own. In the weeks after Jamie's death, the law enforcement family came closer together. Many officers reminisced about a proud father who brought an energetic toddler to the station to be babysat by all. This memory allowed everyone to focus on the joy that Jamie brought with him, and his family's pride. The extent of the loss was captured when a lifelong friend of the Roussey family, Brandon Bearde, told Jamie's father, "They killed my boy." Every day since, Lt. Fred Roussey pins on his badge and goes to work, doing the same thing his son did, knowing full well all the dangers and loss it could entail, in order to protect the citizens of Baltimore.

Police Officer Kevon M. Gavin, Sr.

April 21, 2000, Southwestern District
6 years of service

In the year 2000 alone, the Baltimore Police Department would lose four officers in the line of duty, and in every case an automobile collision would be the cause of death. In March, as Officer Jamie Roussey was passing through an intersection on his way to assist a fellow officer, his patrol car was struck broadside. In October, Sgt. John Platt and Officer Kevin McCarthy would be taken by the carelessness of a drunken driver. The case of Officer Kevon M. Gavin differed in one very significant respect: the collision was a deliberate act of murder.

On the night of April 21, 2000, Eric Stennet left his house with murder on his mind. He strapped on a bulletproof vest, armed himself with a 10mm. Colt semi-automatic pistol and drove to the corner of South Payson and Eagle Streets. The previous week he had sprayed the very same corner with gunfire in an effort to take over a lucrative open-air drug market. Because of his rash acts of violence, a specialized undercover unit was performing surveillance. True to form, Stennet drove up in a Ford Bronco and shot indiscriminately out the window. As citizens dove for cover, Stennet sped off. After ensuring that no one had been injured, the undercover officers gave chase

Other officers joined in pursuit of one of the city's most dangerous criminals. Officer Gavin was one of those who heard the call for assistance and went to assist. Realizing that the pursuit was headed in his direction, he parked his patrol car on Lombard Street in a way that would help protect citizens. Independent witnesses later testified that Stennet accelerated and steered his truck directly into Gavin's vehicle. The crash was horrific, and Stennet's large truck came to rest on top of Officer Gavin's car. Despite the efforts of police and citizens on the scene who worked feverishly to help him, Officer Gavin's wounds proved fatal, and he succumbed to them at the University of Maryland Hospital's Shock Trauma Unit.

Kevon had spent many years in the service of his country and his community, and had given much of himself to ensure that his family was well cared for. After graduating from high school, he decided on a career in the navy to best provide for his younger brother Michael and his mother, who suffered from multiple sclerosis. He served as a radio specialist aboard a navy cruiser during the Persian Gulf War and promised to return to rescue his family from poverty and their drug-ridden neighborhood in New York City. Unfortunately, his mother died in 1991, at the age of thirty-eight, leaving him as the sole support of his younger brother. Making good on his promise, he and Michael moved to Baltimore to make a better life for themselves. He married Lisa Dorsey in 1999 and was soon the proud father of

Kevon Jr. When he married, he took on two stepchildren, eight-year-old Amber, and five-year-old Shawn and loved them as his own. "[My brother] had a big impact on my life and its direction. He made me more goal-oriented and taught me how to make the right decisions in life," said Michael Gavin.

Sergeant John D. Platt

October 14, 2000, Northeastern District
17 years of service

Police Officer Kevin J. McCarthy

October 14, 2000, Northeastern District
15 years of service

Sergeant John Platt rode in the passenger seat as Officer Kevin McCarthy drove eastbound near the intersection of Glenmore and Alta Avenues. Although nothing unusual was happening at that point, they were on a special detail working to stop a string of robberies in the area. The two had driven this road many times before, and each time the route turned their thoughts to their good friend, Lt. Owen Sweeney. Burdick Park and the memorial in his honor were only about a block away. The memorial held special meaning for them. Almost three years earlier, the three had responded together to a call to control a violent, mentally deranged man. Sweeney and Sergeant Platt were in the house attempting to calm the man when a shotgun blast tore through the second floor bedroom door and fatally wounded Sweeney in the back. Owen Sweeney had fallen into the arms of his friend John Platt and had died a short time later.

On the night of October 14, 2000, Sergeant Platt rode with Officer McCarthy as they sought the rogue armed robber who was holding this neighborhood in thrall. It was approximately 7:25 P.M. and they were driving at a leisurely pace down Glenmore Avenue slowly enough to observe suspicious activity, when a speeding, southbound pickup truck driven by an inebriated Shane D. Weiss, bore down on the intersection of Glenmore and Alta Avenues. Weiss, who was moving at well above the posted speed limit (estimated by investigators to be nearly sixty miles per hour), never touched the brakes as he went through the stop sign at the intersection. The sound of the crash seemed to hang in the air forever. The impact destroyed the structural integrity of the driver's side of the police car, throwing it into the air and into a telephone pole.

Arriving firefighters worked feverishly to cut the roof from the car in order to get to the men and provide medical assistance. When medics finally reached Platt and McCarthy it was too late. The impact had taken their lives almost instantly. McCarthy was taken to Good Samaritan Hospital and Platt to Johns Hopkins Bayview Medical Center. Sergeant Platt was a seventeen-year veteran, married to Laurie, with a four-year-old son, John Jr., and a three-year-old daughter, Rachel. Officer McCarthy was a fifteen-year veteran with a nine-year-old daughter, Jessica.

John Platt had grand plans for his retirement less than three years away. He was converting his basement into office space for a private business. He was a man who worked hard to remove criminals from the streets, plastering wanted posters as he walked a foot beat and organizing special squads to hunt them down. His District Commander, Major Tomczak, described him as a caring person who knew when to get tough. His strong desire to fight crime and his obvious dedication to his job made him a welcome and valuable member of the community, many of whom referred to him as "Mr. John." His love for his job, his neighborhood, and his city was unquestioned.

Equally dedicated to family and career was Kevin McCarthy. With fifteen years on the force, he was known to take care of the younger officers as they acclimated themselves to the tough job of policing. Especially touched by Kevin's kindness to younger officers was rookie Regina C. Averella. Assigned to an all-male squad, Regina remembers how Kevin took her under his wing and helped her along through tough times. He cared most about helping his fellow officers reach their full potential as police officers. His standards were high, and he was especially known for his meticulousness when it came to maintaining his patrol car, which stood out from the rest on the station house lot. It was never less than perfectly clean, and when an officer on the previous shift tried to turn it over to McCarthy with trash inside, he refused to accept it until the garbage was removed. Out of the public eye, Kevin worked even harder for his family. When his mother became ill, he used his personal time to clean houses so she would not lose her clients. At a local bank where he provided security, he walked employees to their cars to ensure their safety. But he was best known for his love and devotion to his daughter. Above everything else, raising Jessica was what he cared about most.

Police Agent Michael A. Cowdery, Jr.

March 12, 2001, Eastern District
4 years and 8 months of service

Heavy rain poured onto the shoulders of Officer Ronald Beverly as he stared down the sights of his pistol at the man who had just shot his friend. Moments before, Officers Beverly, Tiffany Walker, Robert Jackson, and Agent Michael Cowdery had gathered at the corner of Cliftview Avenue and Harford Road, investigating young men in a drug and crime-ridden neighborhood. Despite the cold and driving rain they went about their business stifling a small part of the drug trade in this city. They had just interrupted a drug transaction, and the atmosphere was tense.

As they stood on that corner, Howard Whitworth walked toward them with a loaded .357 magnum. When he got close enough, he leveled his weapon at Agent Cowdery and fired twice, killing him instantly. Immediately, Walker and Beverly returned fire but missed their target as Whitworth ran down Cliftview Avenue. Officer Beverly raced after him and a gun battle began. As the bullets flew, Beverly felt a sharp, burning pain in his leg. Despite having been shot he continued to run after Whitworth, caught up to him, and shot him in the side. Whitworth surrendered and was arrested. One year later, Howard Whitworth was sentenced to life in prison without the possibility of parole.

Usually, on a night with a cold rain, officers can count on an easy, slow shift, but this night had an unusual feel. Fifteen minutes before Agent Cowdery was shot, there had been a signal thirteen in the

Northern District as an officer fought another drug dealer in a darkened alley. Officers continue to work hard to safeguard citizens regardless of the weather, and Agent Cowdery was one of the hardest working of all. He had been part of the Eastern District Initiative, a unit that was charged with reducing both violent crime and drug activity in the hardest areas to crack in Baltimore City.

As good as he was, police work was not what defined Michael Cowdery. Called "Baby Face" by his fellow officers and "Mickey" by his family, he was intelligent, polite, and described as reserved by his friends. Before he began a career in policing, he had used his degree in Economics from Hampton University and worked as a financial consultant. He was also known for his patience and strove to emulate his father, a Philadelphia police officer. As a child he watched his father prepare for duty and tugged at his handcuffs to help him straighten the wrinkles in his shirt.

On March 17, 2001, with the spires of the Cathedral of Mary Our Queen reaching high into the gray overcast clouds and cold, steady drizzle, family, friends, and fellow officers packed the cathedral in a show of respect for a man who had put himself willingly in danger to safeguard the lives of people he did not know. To those in attendance, Major Elfago Moye read from a poem that epitomized Michael Cowdery's life: "I go where others fear to go, I did what others failed to do."

Police Officer Crystal D. Sheffield

August 22, 2002, Western District
3 years of service

The most important thing in Crystal Sheffield's life was family. Whether her police family or her immediate family, she did whatever it took whenever help was needed. The Sheffield family is deeply rooted in the Baltimore City Fire and Police departments. Her husband William, now a lieutenant, is a long-time member of the fire department. At the time of her death, her brother, Officer Frederick Allen, worked for the Community Relations Division. Her sister, Maj. Barbara Magness, works in Juvenile Detention, and brother-in-law James Magness is a member of the police department's Inspections Section.

Sharing the characteristics of her family, she was known for her levelheaded approach to police work. She could balance an aggressive approach to policing with the resourcefulness to do the best she could with what she had at hand. Possessed of the ability to handle volatile situations, she rarely had trouble calming arguments among citizens who called the police to solve their problems. What she liked doing most was taking criminals off the street. One of her side partners, Robert Jones, recalled many times when she assisted fellow officers arresting violent offenders. "We went into a lot of dark alleys together," he recalled. Placing fear aside, she worked hard to make sure her fellow officers were safe. While she was on duty, everyone knew that a backup officer was just moments away.

On the night of August 21, 2002, a frantic call for assistance from one of her fellow officers was broadcast over the radio, and she reacted immediately. She turned on her lights and siren, just as she had many times before, and headed for the scene—the intersection of Baltimore and Carey Streets, where her fellow officer was trying to control a crowd. She was driving east on Lafayette, but because of her siren and the busy city streets, she never heard or saw the unmarked police car southbound on Carey Street. She made her turn onto Carey Street and was struck on the driver's side door. The collision resulted in massive internal and head injuries that would prove fatal. Early on the morning of August 22, 2002, she succumbed to her wounds at the University of Maryland's Shock Trauma Center.

Police Officer Crystal Sheffield was the first female officer to be killed in the line of duty, leaving behind her husband and eleven-year-old son Darian. Crystal is best known for her love of family and her dedication to her fellow officers.

Detective Thomas G. Newman

November 23, 2002, Central Investigation Division, Check and Fraud Unit
12 years of service

At 2:30 A.M. on April 21, 2001, Tommy Newman stopped at a South Baltimore gas station to buy a soda for his ride home. Detective Newman of the Warrant Apprehension Task Force had just gotten off duty and was focused on going home to get some rest. He was keeping to himself, as he usually did, when for no apparent reason he became the object of ridicule of four men. Tommy knew that the best course of action was to ignore them and leave. But the men pushed their taunts to the point where Tommy flashed his badge in the hope of diffusing the situation, and to let them know he was tired of the comments. Instead, one of the men made a motion that indicated he was also armed, which raised the tensions further. The four got into their car and drove away. Tommy called for help on his cell phone and tried to follow them at a safe distance, but before help arrived the men had parked their car and fled the scene. Tommy was standing by his truck, talking with a 911 dispatcher, when shots exploded from behind him, one of the bullets striking him in the neck.

Eventually, Andre A. Travers was arrested and charged with the attempted murder of Tommy Newman. The day came for Tommy to take the stand and testify against the man who had so ruthlessly shot him. His voice was low but sure, quiet but confident, and his testimony was the critical evidence that convicted Travers and sent him to a long prison sentence. Although Travers's actions angered a police department that was experiencing a sharp increase in violent attacks on officers, there was some solace in the fact that one more gun and one more violent man was off the street. Not so for the family of the gunman, who focused their rage on Detective Newman.

Detective Newman left his post in the Warrant Task Force after the shooting to join the Check and Fraud Unit. The change in venue introduced Tommy to a group of men and women who would become very close to him, as if they were his own family. In his new position, he dealt with a different class of criminal. People who stole from others by defrauding credit card companies and banks offered a new challenge. Tommy was soon described as "a detective who found his niche." Detective Sergeant Lester McCrea recalled times when the unit came together on particularly tough cases and collectively sorted through mounds of evidence to discover the common threads. With a head for making connections with numbers and an uncanny ability to illicit confessions, Tommy continually impressed his side partners.

Even though his dedication to duty was evident, Tommy had another side, his devotion to family, that many never knew. The Check and Fraud Unit is one unit within the department that keeps a fairly regular schedule, a benefit that officers accustomed to shift work with rotating schedules envy. Tommy used this schedule to do something that many others could not fathom. After an often exhausting day of tediously tracking down financial records, he worked long into the night maintaining his family farm in Upper Marlboro. Though often tired, Tommy never complained. "Every once in a while," Sergeant McCrea said, "you might see Tommy sitting at his desk in obvious pain. He would never let anyone know it, but the bullet that remained in his neck would send shocks throughout his body."

One evening eighteen months after he had been shot, Tommy took a break and visited a local bar with his girlfriend. He had no idea that the half-brother of the man who had tried to kill him was in the same bar. As Tommy relaxed and socialized, Raymond Saunders left to find Jovan House and Anthony Brown—to plan the execution of a police officer.

The end came soon after, when Tommy walked out of Joe's and into the street. Detective Newman was always prepared for anything, but no amount of preparation could have stopped the ambush that awaited him this night—a hail of bullets fired at nearly point-blank range into his chest from men he did not know. Tommy collapsed in the street with a bullet lodged in his heart, the victim of a senseless act by people who held no value for human life. A security officer who witnessed the shooting chased the three, shooting as he drove, but could not apprehend them. Eventually they were caught, and before a courtroom packed with uniformed police officers, Saunders, House, and Brown were convicted and sentenced to join the original shooter for lengthy prison terms.

Prison sentences bring a form of closure to the friends and family of officers killed in the line of duty, but true healing comes in the bonding among all of those who held Tommy close to their hearts. Detective Newman left behind two children, a six-year-old son and a three-year-old daughter, and a large immediate family. "Tommy's family is now our family," Sergeant McCrea said. "We celebrate birthdays together, we remember together, we heal together."

Lieutenant Walter A. Taylor

April 17, 2003, Eastern District
36 years and 5 months of service

The rule was made many years ago, among Lt. Walter A. Taylor's close circle of friends, that whenever their conversations turned to the most respected leaders of the Baltimore Police Department and Commissioner Donald D. Pomerleau's name was mentioned, they would stand and salute. When Walt Taylor joined the department in November 1966, his academy class was one of the first to be hired under Commissioner Pomerleau. Like many men and women from that period of Baltimore's policing history, Walt's respect for one of its greatest leaders was eternal. He credited the commissioner with bringing the department out of a Stone Age of equipment and tactics, in the process building the highest morale the department had ever known, and referred to him as "the Father of the Modern Baltimore Police Department."

With this early exposure to great leadership, he made every effort to emulate those he respected. Over the course of more than thirty-six years, Walt became an admired leader in his own right. Born and raised in Howard County, he heeded the call for public service just after graduating from Howard High School. He joined the Howard County Fire Department as one of its first paid ambulance drivers and married his high school sweetheart, Betsy. He then decided that he wanted to be a police officer and with her support joined the force.

After spending time in the Southwestern District he was promoted to sergeant in 1974, and worked in the Southern and Central Districts before being promoted again, this time to lieutenant, in 1981. It was early in 1983 that he discovered one of his true loves of policing, the Tactical Section. For nine years he commanded "B" Platoon in the Quick Response Team, then led the Aviation Unit for three years. While serving in these positions of command, he earned numerous awards and accolades. Even though he had much about which to boast, he was known as a humble man and an "old-school-cop," who made sure that his first priority was always the men and women who served under him.

In 1995 he was transferred from the Aviation Unit to the Eastern District to take charge as a shift commander because of a short-lived policy known as "rotation." Walt took the assignment as a challenge and tackled many roles during his return to Patrol. He maintained the highest standards for himself and those who worked with and for him. Those in his district knew that he expected consistently high performance and little use of sick leave. Never a complainer himself, he always led by example, even taking vacation time rather than sick leave to have a pacemaker inserted to correct a heart condition about which few people knew.

Eventually, he was given the responsibility of the Administrative and Inspections Lieutenant. In early April 2003, he began to prepare for his turn to present at a highly stressful meeting known as "Comstat." It was well known throughout the department that Comstat could be brutal. An unrelenting command staff was known to humiliate those who were slow to answer or give wrong answers to their intense scrutiny. For the entire week prior to his presentation, Walt worked feverishly. He spent his time at the District Station House researching, interviewing his fellow lieutenants and sergeants, and hounding those around him for statistics for proof of crime prevention and enforcement. At home he continued his preparation by planning and studying. On the day of his presentation he was prepared. His answers to tough questions were honest and forthright, demonstrating his pride in his district and those who worked there. He returned to his office afterward and settled into his office chair. Several hours later, Officer Adrienne Gillis walked into Walt's office and found him still in his chair and unresponsive. He had died of a heart attack.

After a career that stretched nearly four decades, he had been looking forward to a peaceful retirement. He had plans to restore a 1955 Chevrolet and take his grandsons to NASCAR events, and he most wanted to spend time on the big family vacations that he had enjoyed throughout his life with Betsy and his daughter, Heather. Controversy immediately surrounded his death. Although the heart attack was indisputable, the cause was at issue. After more than a year of investigation, his death was ruled to be in the line of duty, that the stress of his preparation and presentation at Comstat were the immediate causes of his heart attack. With this direct causal relationship established, Walt's name is honored as it should be, alongside those of his department's fallen heroes.

Police Officer Brian D. Winder

July 3, 2004, Southwestern District
9 years and 9 months of service

Silence permeated the Southwestern District station house for days after Officer Brian Winder was shot to death outside a liquor store in the 4600 block of Edmondson Avenue. It was as though the men and women who worked alongside Brian all hoped to wake up from a horrible nightmare and see him back in the roll call room, laughing and joking as he always had. But the incident was all too real, and grief made the simplest tasks difficult. Some pondered their own mortality while others did what they could to comfort those who had been hit the hardest. Brian Winder had symbolized everything that was right with the department and the city he loved. He was kind, funny, and honest. He was proud to work in the neighborhood in which he grew up, and he was proud to wear the uniform of the Baltimore City Police Department. Like many on the force, Brian wanted to help the young boys and girls who played on the same streets he had as a child.

On the night of July 3, 2004, at 8:40 in the evening, he received a call for a domestic disturbance in Edmondson Village. A woman was having a difficult time dealing with Jermaine Gaines. After a severe argument Gaines had left the scene with a handgun in his waistband. Officer Winder arrived just after Gaines had left the area and listened to the frightened woman's story. She feared Gaines and pleaded with Officer Winder to find him and make sure he stayed away from her home. Brian promised to do his best. Only a few minutes had passed since Gaines had left, so Brian immediately went out to find him.

Gaines had met a friend, Charles Bennett, and they decided to go to G&G Liquors on Edmondson Avenue. Bennett, like Gaines, was a violent convicted felon, on this night armed with a handgun. The two were standing in front of the liquor store when Brian slowed to a stop in front of them. Officer Winder recognized the pair and told them to stay where they were. Other officers on patrol in the area heard Brian call out over the radio, asking them to respond. In such a violent area with an officer like Brian asking for help, several answered the request. He stepped from his car and the two men turned and walked back inside the store. When Brian entered behind them, gunshots rang out. Unable to draw his weapon Brian sought anyplace that offered protection. He stumbled out onto the sidewalk, shouting "Shots fired!" on his radio before falling to the ground a short distance from the door. He had been hit five times.

Officer Ed Lane was the first to arrive to back up his mortally wounded friend. Lane pulled his weapon and cornered Gaines as he retreated back into the liquor store, trying to hide the weapon he was carrying. Charles Bennett, the man who had fired the shots, escaped. While Gaines was handcuffed, Officer Tomecha Johnson arrived and tried to provide aid and comfort. Before the ambulance arrived, Tomecha held her friend in her arms and prayed for a miracle. Brian was pronounced dead in the emergency room at Shock Trauma.

During Gaines's interrogation, homicide detectives learned Bennett's identity and his role in the course of events. Within hours an arrest warrant was issued. A massive hunt involving dozens of anonymous tips was underway. The city's best were called upon to find the officer's killer. Bennett's picture was plastered throughout police stations across the city and broadcast on the local television news. Finally a tip paid off. Bennett, using a false name, had checked himself into a cheap hotel called the Relax Inn. The Quick Response

Team suited up and began a systematic search of the hotel. The heavily armed officers cleared room after room, working their way from the top floor to the bottom. When the knock went unanswered for room number 205, the lead officer opened the door with a master key and the team heard a shot. Bennett had placed the same gun he had used to kill Brian against his own head and pulled the trigger.

The death of the suspect brought mixed feelings to all of those involved, relief that he had been found and frustration that he could not be made to pay for his crime with a lifelong prison sentence. Comfort, however, came in the form of fond memories of a great officer. At his funeral on July 9, stories of an energetic man who had danced the night away at a friend's wedding only a week before, slowly replaced grief and a sense of despair. His wife, Lorrie, stepdaughter Kimberly, and sons Corey and Brandon found their strength and support in their large family. But the words of a child would provide the greatest comfort of all. "It's OK," seven-year-old Jeremiah Stokes told Mayor Martin O'Malley. "He's an angel." "Perhaps he always was," the mayor replied.

Sergeant Anthony A. Byrd

May 19, 2006, Southwestern District
11 years, 1 month service

In the early morning hours of May 19, 2006, an officer assigned to the Accident Investigation Unit began to gather information in the twisted metal and shattered glass strewn across the intersection of Stafford Street and Parksley Avenue. He sprayed bright orange paint on the ground beneath two police cars, marking the positions where they had come to rest after a violent collision. The evidence would tell the story of events leading to this crash that ended with the death of a beloved family member, friend, father, and husband.

The conclusion of the investigation, which involved the skills of a seasoned accident reconstructionist, revealed what was entirely too clear at the scene. Officer Anthony "Tony" A. Byrd's car had been struck broadside by that of another police officer who was responding to a call for service. By the time either officer saw the other it was too late. The initial impact drove Tony's car across the street and into a telephone pole directly on the driver's side door.

Calls for assistance were immediate, and help was on scene within moments. While fire department personnel cut away the doors and roof to Tony's car, all his friends could do was wait and pray. Tony believed strongly in the power of prayer and was a devout Christian. Some would believe that their prayers went unanswered that night when he was pronounced dead at St. Agnes Hospital nearly forty minutes later. Tony's fellow officers were nearly overwhelmed by the sudden loss of a very good friend.

After the crash, Officer Byrd's car was towed to the Central Garage Body Shop with a black tarp covering it. The car's twisted body sobered the conversation of all who had saw it and served as a reminder that time is always precious. Those closest to Tony would rely on their faith and trust in God to help them through such a difficult period.

Tony's death marked the second time in less than two years that the Southwestern District had lost an officer. Brian Winder had been shot to death outside of a liquor store on Edmondson Avenue in July 2004. The men and women of this station knew the pain of loss all to well. Once again, the uniform badges and decals on patrol vehicles bore the traditional black band that signifies the death of an officer in the line of duty.

Although death in the line of duty is relatively commonplace in law enforcement, each and every instance brings to light the willingness of some of society's best citizens to lay down their lives to protect others. Because of the frequent possibility of serious harm, the culture of police departments is intimate and exclusive. Men and women who wear the badge consider one another to be family regardless of whatever differences may be apparent to outsiders. This type of closeness is well established among all members of the Baltimore Police Department and is much more visible on the District level.

As they did with Brian Winder, the officers of the Southwestern District banded together and became even closer. In a newsletter published by the Department, Freddie Degraffinried said, "If tears could bring my friend back . . . you would have about a million Tonys." Although they would much prefer that nothing like this ever occur, Tony's brothers and sisters in uniform know that he would rejoice in a deeper faith and closeness that his death has established. Officer Byrd, who had been scheduled for promotion to sergeant, received his promotion posthumously.

Detective Troy Lamont Chesley, Sr.

January 9, 2007, Public Housing Unit, 13 years of service

The posters and flyers once again appeared on locker room walls and station house cork boards announcing that another officer's family needed help to make it through the toughest time. Their appearance marks the frustration and sense of loss that fills the days, weeks, months, and years after an officer is killed in the line of duty.

These reminded all that Detective Troy "T-Roy" Chesley had children and a family who were now without a father, and asked for donations of any kind. Officers who know that nothing can be done to bring their friends back promise once again, to "never forget." And they won't, ever.

Troy Chesley knew first hand the rewards of serving a specific neighborhood. For years he worked diligently as an undercover officer for the Public Housing Unit to bring peace to an area dominated by violence and drugs. He believed in Baltimore and knew the importance of his work. Troy was going home early in the morning of January 9, 2007, to a house in the 4500 block of Fairfax Road. He was on the front porch, just about to open his door.

From behind him came a voice. It was that of a seasoned, hardened criminal who had chosen a life of violence and disregard for others—twenty-one-year-old Brandon Grimes, whose contempt for law and order was obvious as he initiated a robbery that would soon turn deadly. Grimes had no way of knowing that the man he approached with his pistol in hand was a police officer. Grimes was no stranger to jail, and the prospect of punishment did not deter him from preying on those who were honest and decent. With seventeen arrests and several convictions, Grimes was currently walking the streets after posting a $500,000 bail for his second handgun arrest in as many years.

Troy managed to get to his weapon in an attempt to protect himself, but when the fusillade of shots ended both men had been hit. Troy's wounds were fatal; he died only a few feet from the safety of his house. Grimes ran from the scene with a wound gushing blood, leaving a lengthy trail down the block's sidewalk. Eventually detectives recovered the gun used to kill Troy along this trail and found his killer seeking treatment for a near fatal gunshot at St. Agnes Hospital in South Baltimore. The bullet in Grimes's leg would furnish definitive proof that it was he who had killed Detective Troy Chesley.

Recalling fond memories is one way to deal with the pain of sudden loss, and many men and women did just that, gathering together and turning their focus to the life of Troy Chesley. They told reporters and outsiders of lighter moments in ping pong games, of Troy's heroic efforts to save people from burning buildings, and his quiet, reflective personality. In private moments, other feelings surfaced. One officer paused as he went about the daily business of policing and said: "I've lost a friend, a partner, and I don't think I'll ever be able to wrap my brain around that."

Troy's children, Troy Jr., fourteen, Tavon, twelve, Ryan, twelve, Chastity twelve, and Raven, six, have every reason to be proud of their dad. Many men and women take the oath to serve and protect their fellow citizens, but few did it quite as well as Troy did. It is the life, not the circumstances surrounding the death, of Troy Chesley that will be remembered by his friends, family, and fellow officers. In attempting to rob a man of a few dollars, Brandon Grimes robbed a community of a favored son.

APPENDICES

Appendix A

Officers by District

Central / Middle District

Officer	Page
George Workner	3
William Jourdan	7
Joseph C. Clark	12
James T. Dunn	21
Michael Neary	21
John Lanahan	29
Carroll Hanley	59
William L. Ryan	64
William J. Woodcock	65
Fred R. Unger	71
Henry Smith, Jr.	98
Edward J. Kowalewski	101
Francis R. Stransky	103
Henry M. Mickey	121
Donald W. Sager	123
Carl Peterson, Jr.	125
Edgar J. Rumpf	147
William J. Martin	166
Herman A. Jones, Sr.	171
Harold J. Carey	177

Southeastern District

Officer	Page
George F. Heim	120
Lorenzo A. Gray	128
Calvin M. Rodwell	134
Gerald M. Arminger	173

Eastern District

Officer	Page
John O'Mayer	5
Charles Fisher	17
George C. Sauer	26
Frank L. Latham	30
James L. Scholl	82
Walter P. Matthys	106
William J. Baumer	114
Frank W. Whitby, Jr.	135
Milton I. Spell	139
William D. Albers	153
Vincent J. Adolfo	161
Michael A. Cowdery, Jr.	187
Walter Taylor	193

NORTHEASTERN DISTRICT

Charles J. Donohue	25
John Blank	51
John T. King, Jr.	60
Thomas J. Barlow	62
William S. Knight	67
Elmer A. Noon	69
Walter D. Davis	86
Jack L. Cooper	109
Robert M. Hurley	130
Owen E. Sweeney, Jr.	175
John D. Platt	184
Kevin J. McCarthy	184

NORTHERN DISTRICT

Henry Sudmeier	55
Joseph D. Benedict	73
James L. Joyce	76
Roland W. Morgan	80
Frederick K. Kontner	116
John C. Williams	117
Martin J. Greiner	141
Richard J. Lear	158

NORTHWESTERN DISTRICT

Webster E. Schuman	36
Thomas J. Dillon	36
William F. Doehler	38
John P. Burns	44
William A. Bell	46
John A. Stapf	54
Arthur H. Malinofski	57
John W. Arnold	75
Aubrey L. Lowman	84
James J. Purcell	87
John R. Phelan	90
Richard H. Duvall, Jr.	95
Teddy L. Bafford	108
Norman F. Buchman	132

WESTERN DISTRICT

Benjamin Benton	8
Robert M. Rigdon	8
James Murphy	11
John Christopher	15
Alonzo B. Bishop	23
Claude J. Profili	104
Charles R. Ernest	110
Robert H. Kuhn	112
Jimmy D. Halcomb	146
Ronald L. Tracey	155
Ira N. Weiner	168
Jamie Roussey	181
Crystal D. Sheffield	189

SOUTHWESTERN DISTRICT

Thomas F. Steinacker	48
Edward S. Sherman	143
Timothy B. Ridnour	144
Robert Alexander	165
Kevon M. Gavin, Sr.	182
Brian Winder	196
Anthony A. Byrd	198

SOUTHERN DISTRICT

John T. Lloyd	19
Jacob Zapp	20
John J. Dailey	22
Charles S. Frank	32
George M. J. May	40
John R. J. Block	49
Max Hirsch	56
John B. Bealefeld	68
Alfred P. Bobelis	83
Martin E. Webb	127

AVIATION UNIT

Barry W. Wood	179

Appendix B

Calendar Index

January 1, 1925	George D. Hart
January 2, 1932	William A. Bell
January 6, 1884	Charles W. Fisher
January 6, 1951	Roland Morgan
January 7, 1931	John P. Burns
January 9, 2007	Troy Lamont Chesley
January 10, 1964	Francis Stransky
January 11, 1959	Richard Duvall
January 13, 1947	Fred Unger
January 16, 1970	George Heim
January 20, 1965	Charles R. Ernest
January 25, 1967	William Baumer
February 6, 1964	Claude Profili
February 10, 1967	Frederick K. Kontner
February 11, 1934	John Blank
February 12, 1928	George M. J. May
February 13, 1948	Joseph Benedict
February 14, 1935	Max Hirsh
February 14, 1954	Alfred P. Bobelis
February 15, 1978	Edgar J. Rumpf
March 2, 1924	Frank Latham
March 8, 2000	Jamie Roussey
March 12, 2001	Michael Cowdery Jr.

March 15, 1808	George Workner
March 24, 1970	Henry Mickey
March 29, 1973	Robert M. Hurley
April 4, 1949	James L. Joyce
April 6, 1973	Norman Buchman
April 7, 1962	Henry Smith Jr.
April 16, 1976	Jimmy D. Halcomb
April 17, 2003	Walter Taylor
April 18, 1968	Richard Bosak
April 18, 1915	George C. Sauer
April 19, 1954	Aubrey L. Lowman
April 21, 1933	John R. J. Block
April 21, 2000	Kevon M. Gavin
April 23, 1978	Robert J. Barlow
April 24, 1970	Donald Sager
May 5, 1974	Frank Whitby Jr.
May 7, 1997	Owen E. Sweeney Jr.
May 19, 2006	Anthony Byrd
May 20, 1902	Charles Donohue
May 22, 1871	Joseph Clark
May 26, 1962	Richard Seebo
May 26, 1993	Herman A. Jones Sr.
June 12, 1971	Carl Peterson Jr.
June 13, 1940	William L. Ryan
June 13, 1943	William J. Woodcock
June 20, 1894	James T. Dunn
June 20, 1894	Michael Neary
June 20, 1924	Charles F. Frank
June 24, 1994	George M. Arminger

June 29, 1926	Webster Schuman
July 1, 1954	Walter D. Davis
July 2, 1962	Edward Kowalewski
July 3, 1919	John Lanahan
July 3, 2004	Brian D. Winder
July 4, 1889	John T. Lloyd
July 5, 1870	James Murphy
July 12, 1926	Thomas Dillon
July 15, 1891	Jacob Zapp
July 20, 1981	Ronald L. Tracey
July 21, 1986	Richard T. Miller
July 22, 1965	Robert H. Kuhn
July 26, 1972	Lorenzo A. Gray
August 1, 1953	James L. Scholl
August 1, 1971	Martin E. Webb
August 1, 1974	Frank Grunder Jr.
August 4, 1950	Charles Hilbert
August 5, 1927	William Doehler
August 15, 1974	Milton I. Spell
August 19, 1979	William D. Albers
August 21, 1967	John C. Williams
August 23, 1872	John Christopher
August 22, 2002	Crystal D. Sheffield
August 29, 1899	Alonzo B. Bishop
September 4, 1871	John Richards
September 10, 1945	John Bealefeld
September 11, 1964	Walter Matthys
September 13, 1975	Edward Sherman
September 14, 1871	John H. Richards
September 19, 1958	Robert K. Nelson

September 20, 1986	Robert Alexander
September 21, 1992	Ira N. Weiner
September 22, 1858	Benjamin Benton
September 22, 1973	Calvin Rodwell
September 29, 1956	John R. Phelan
October 1, 1948	Thomas Burns
October 4, 1932	Thomas Steinacker
October 8, 1985	Richard J. Lear
October 9, 1936	Leo Bacon
October 9, 1957	John F. Andrews
October 10, 1989	William J. Martin
October 14, 1857	William Jourdan
October 14, 2000	Kevin J. McCarthy
October 14, 2000	John D. Platt
October 15, 1964	Teddy Bafford
October 16, 1949	Thomas J. O'Neill
October 17, 1895	John J. Dailey
October 24, 1955	James J. Purcell
October 27, 1975	Timothy B. Ridnour
October 27, 1978	Nelson F. Bell Jr.
October 29, 1936	Carroll Hanley
October 30, 1998	Harold J. Carey
October 31, 1935	Arthur Malinofski
November 1, 1925	Roy L. Mitchell
November 1, 1938	Joseph Keene
November 2, 1934	John A. Stapf
November 4, 1998	Barry W. Wood
November 5, 1858	Robert M. Rigdon
November 7, 1943	William Knight
November 14, 1856	John O'Mayer

November 16, 1960	Warren V. Eckert
November 18, 1985	Vincent J. Adolfo
November 19, 1928	Joseph F. Carroll
November 20, 1946	Elmer A. Noon
November 23, 2002	Thomas G. Newman
December 3, 1984	Marcellus Ward
December 10, 1974	Martin Greiner
December 20, 1934	Henry Sudmeier
December 25, 1964	Jack L. Cooper
December 28, 1936	John T. King
December 30, 1948	John W. Arnold
December 31, 1937	Thomas J. Barlow

APPENDIX C

Alphabetical Roll of Officers

References

Night Watchman George Workner
Baltimore American & Commercial Dailey Advertiser, 15 March–23 April 1808; *Baltimore Whig*, 17 March–28 April 1808; J. Thomas Scharf, *Chronicles of Baltimore* (Baltimore: Turnbull Brothers, 1874); Court Records of Trial, State v. Doherty, C183, Maryland State Archives, Annapolis.

Night Watchman John O'Mayer
Baltimore American & Commercial Daily Advertiser, 3–16 November 1856; Tracy Matthew Melton, *Hanging Henry Gambrill: The Violent Career of Baltimore's Plug Uglies 1854–1860* (Baltimore: Maryland Historical Society, 2005).

Sergeant William Jourdan
Baltimore Sun, 15–19 October 1857, 3–5 February 1859; Melton, *Hanging Henry Gambrill: The Violent Career of Baltimore's Plug Uglies 1854–1860;* Court Records of Trial, State v. McFarland, Maryland State Archives.

Patrolmen Benjamin Benton and Robert Rigdon
Baltimore Sun, 24 September–8 November 1858, 5 January–10 February 1859, 9 April 1859; Melton, *Hanging Henry Gambrill: The Violent Career of Baltimore's Plug Uglies 1854–1860*; Scharf, *Chronicles of Baltimore*; Court Records of Trial, State v. Gambrill, C1849, Maryland State Archives.

Patrolman James Murphy
Baltimore Sun, 6–9 July 1870 and 31 May 1871; Court Records of Trial, State v. Duering. Maryland State Archives C1849-43; Official Personnel Jacket, Baltimore Police Central Records Department.

Patrolman Joseph C. Clark
Baltimore Sun, 23 May–8 June and 1–2 November 1871; Court Records of Trial, State v. Kussey. Maryland State Archives C92-3; Baltimore City Indictment Book. Maryland State Archives C1849-46; Official Personnel Jacket, Baltimore Police Central Records Department.

Detective John H. Richards
Baltimore American Commercial Daily Advertiser, 1–18 September 1871; *Baltimore Sun,* 1–19 September 1871; Official Personnel Jacket, Baltimore Police Central Records Department.

Patrolman John Christopher
Baltimore Sun, 20–26 August 1872; Official Personnel Jacket, Baltimore Police Central Records Department.

Patrolman Charles W. Fisher
Baltimore News-American, 7–9 January 1884; *Baltimore Sun,* 7–9 January 1884; *Washington Post,* 7 January 1884; Official Personnel Jacket, Baltimore Police Central Records Department; Death Certificate, Maryland State Archives, CR49,109, Certificate # 72 305.

Patrolman John T. Lloyd
Baltimore News-American, 4–8 July 1889; *Baltimore Sun,* 4–8 July 1889; Official Personnel Jacket, Baltimore Police Central Records Department; Death Certificate, Maryland State Archives, Certificate # 18584.

Patrolman Jacob Zapp
Baltimore News-American, 16 July 1891; *Baltimore Sun,* 16–17 July 1891; Official Personnel Jacket, Baltimore Police Central Records Department; Death Certificate, Maryland State Archives, Certificate # 38345.

Patrolmen James T. Dunn and Michael Neary
Baltimore News-American, 21 June 1894; *Baltimore Sun,* 21–25 June 1894; Official Personnel Jacket, Baltimore Police Central Records Department; Death Certificate, Maryland State Archives, Certificate # 6775; Death Certificate, Maryland State Archives, Certificate # 6776.

Patrolman John J. Dailey
Baltimore News-American, 26 August–18 October 1895; *Baltimore Sun,* 27 August–18 October 1895; Official Personnel Jacket, Baltimore Police Central Records Department; Baltimore City Indictment Book. Maryland State Archives. C1849-104.

Patrolman Alonzo B. Bishop
Baltimore News-American, 25–29 August 1899; *Baltimore Sun,* 25–30 August 1899; Official Personnel Jacket, Baltimore Police Central Records Department; Death Certificate, Maryland State Archives, Certificate # 19913.

Patrolman Charles J. Donohue
Baltimore News-American, 21–28 May 1902; *Baltimore Sun,* 20–24 May 1902; Baltimore City Indictment Book. Maryland State Archives. C1849-111; Official Personnel Jacket, Baltimore Police Central Records Department.

Patrolman George C. Sauer
Baltimore News-American, 9–19 April 1915; *Baltimore Sun,* 9–20 April 1915; August Gribbin, *How It All Happened* (New York: Vantage Press, 1980); Baltimore City Indictment Book, Maryland State Archives, C1849-124; Official Personnel Jacket, Baltimore Police Central Records Department; Death Certificate, Maryland State Archives, Certificate # C84653.

Patrolman John Lanahan
Baltimore News-American, 3–4 July 1919; *Baltimore Sun,* 3–4 July 1919; Official Personnel Jacket, Baltimore Police Central Records Department; Death Certificate, Maryland State Archives, Certificate # 33195.

Patrolman Frank L. Latham
Baltimore Evening Sun, 3–7 March 1924; *Baltimore News-American,* 4 March 1924; *Baltimore Sun,* 3–7 March 1924; Official Personnel Jacket, Baltimore Police Central Records Department; Death Certificate, Maryland State Archives, Certificate # 84463.

Patrolman Charles S. Frank
Baltimore Evening Sun, 21–24 June 1924; *Baltimore Sun,* 21–24 June 1924; Official Personnel Jacket, Baltimore Police Central Records Department; Death Certificate, Maryland State Archives, Certificate # 88059.

Patrolman George D. Hart
Baltimore News-American, 17 November 1924; *Baltimore News-American,* 2–3 January 1925; *Baltimore Sun,* 3 January 1925; Official Personnel Jacket, Baltimore Police Central Records Department; Death Certificate, Maryland State Archives, Certificate # 88656.

Patrolman Roy L. Mitchell
Baltimore Sun, 29 October–2 November 1925; Official Personnel Jacket, Baltimore Police Central Records Department; Death Certificate, Maryland State Archives, Certificate # 88381.

Patrolman Webster E. Schuman and Station Clerk Thomas J. Dillon
Baltimore Sun, 29 June–16 July 1926; *Baltimore News-American,* 1–17 July 1926; Official Personnel Jackets, Baltimore Police Central Records Department; Death Certificates, Maryland State Archives, Certificate # 11991 and # 12366.

Patrolman William F. Doehler
Baltimore News-American, 6–10 August 1927; Official Personnel Jacket, Baltimore Police Central Records Department; Death Certificate, Maryland State Archives, Certificate # 24544.

Detective Sergeant Joseph F. Carroll
Baltimore News-American, 19–20 November 1928; *Baltimore Sun,* 20–21 November 1928; Official Personnel Jacket, Baltimore Police Central Records Department; Death Certificate, Maryland State Archives, Certificate # 39408.

Sergeant George M. J. May
Baltimore Sun, 13–15 February 1928; Official Personnel Jacket, Baltimore Police Central Records Department; Death Certificate, Maryland State Archives, Certificate # 30545.

Patrolman John P. Burns
Baltimore News-American, 6–7 January 1931; *Baltimore Sun,* 7–11 January 1931; Official Personnel Jacket, Baltimore Police Central Records Department; Death Certificate, Maryland State Archives, Certificate # E64016.

Patrolman William A. Bell
Baltimore Sun, 3–4 January 1932; Official Personnel Jacket, Baltimore Police Central Records Department; Death Certificate, Maryland State Archives, Certificate # E75417.

Patrolman Thomas F. Steinacker
Baltimore News-American, 28 September 1932; Official Personnel Jacket, Baltimore Police Central Records Department; Death Certificate, Maryland State Archives, Certificate #E83425.

Patrolman John R. J. Block
Baltimore News-American, 22–23 April 1933; *Baltimore Sun,* 22–24 April 1933; Official Personnel Jacket, Baltimore Police Central Records Department; Death Certificate, Maryland State Archives, Certificate #89763.

Patrolman John Blank
Baltimore News-American, 12–16 February 1934; *Baltimore Sun,* 13–14 February 1934; Official Personnel Jacket, Baltimore Police Central Records Department; Death Certificate, Maryland State Archives, Certificate # E98355.

Patrolman John A. Stapf
Baltimore News-American, 3 November 1934; Official Personnel Jacket, Baltimore Police Central Records Department; Death Certificate, Maryland State Archives, Unknown #.

Patrolman Henry Sudmeier
Baltimore Sun, 19–23 October 1926; *Baltimore Sun,* 21 December 1934; Official Personnel Jacket, Baltimore Police Central Records Department; Death Certificate, Maryland State Archives, Certificate # F07634.

Patrolman Max Hirsch
Baltimore Sun, 12–13 February 1935; Official Personnel Jacket, Baltimore Police Central Records Department; Death Certificate, Maryland State Archives, Certificate # E09739.

Patrolman Arthur H. Malinofski
Baltimore Sun, 1–5 November 1935; *Baltimore News-American,* 1–3 November 1935; Official Personnel Jacket, Baltimore Police Central Records Department; Death Certificate, Maryland State Archives, Certificate # F17276.

Patrolman Leo Bacon
Baltimore Sun, 27 February and 10 October, 1932; Official Personnel Jacket, Baltimore Police Central Records Department; Death Certificate, Maryland State Archives, Certificate # F27983.

Patrolman Carroll Hanley
Baltimore Sun, 30 October–3 November 1936; *Baltimore News-American,* 30 October–2 November 1936; Official Personnel Jacket, Baltimore Police Central Records Department; Death Certificate, Maryland State Archives, Certificate # F28625.

Patrolman John T. King, Jr.
Baltimore News-American, 29 December 1936; *Baltimore Sun,* 31 December 1936; Official Personnel Jacket, Baltimore Police Central Records Department; Death Certificate, Maryland State Archives, Certificate # F30585.

Patrolman Thomas J. Barlow
Baltimore Sun, 1 January 1938; Official Personnel Jacket, Baltimore Police Central Records Department; Death Certificate, Maryland State Archives, Certificate # H42143.

Chief Engineer Joseph E. Keene
Baltimore Sun, 2 November 1938; Official Personnel Jacket, Baltimore Police Central Records Department; Death Certificate, Maryland State Archives, Certificate # F54703.

Patrolman William L. Ryan
Baltimore Sun, 14–20 June 1940; Official Personnel Jacket, Baltimore Police Central Records Department; Death Certificate, Maryland State Archives, Certificate # F70243.

Patrolman William J. Woodcock
Baltimore Sun, 14–16 June 1943; *Baltimore News-American,* 14 June 1943; Official Personnel Jacket, Baltimore Police Central Records Department.

Patrolman William S. Knight
Baltimore Sun, 8–10 November 1943; Official Personnel Jacket, Baltimore Police Central Records Department.

Patrolman John B. Bealefeld
Baltimore News-American, 1–11 September 1945; *Baltimore Sun,* 31 August–11 September 1945; Official Personnel Jacket, Baltimore Police Central Records Department.

Patrolman Elmer A. Noon
Baltimore News-American, 21 November 1946; *Baltimore Sun,* 21–22 November 1946; Official Personnel Jacket, Baltimore Police Central Records Department; Death Certificate, Maryland State Archives, Certificate # 4010.

Patrolman Fred R. Unger
Baltimore Sun, 14–17 January 1947; Official Personnel Jacket, Baltimore Police Central Records Department.

Patrolman Joseph D. Benedict
Baltimore Sun, 16–19 October 1949; Official Personnel Jacket, Baltimore Police Central Records Department.

Patrolman Thomas J. Burns
Baltimore Sun, 2 October 1948; Official Personnel Jacket, Baltimore Police Central Records Department.

Patrolman John W. Arnold
Baltimore Sun, 13 December–2 January 1948; Official Personnel Jacket, Baltimore Police Central Records Department.

Patrolman James L. Joyce
Baltimore News-American, 4 April 1949; *Baltimore Sun,* 4–6 April 1949; Official Personnel Jacket, Baltimore Police Central Records Department.

Patrolman Thomas J. O'Neill
Baltimore News-American, 18 October 1949; *Baltimore Sun,* 17 October 1949; Official Personnel Jacket, Baltimore Police Central Records Department; Death Certificate, Maryland State Archives, Certificate # G79008.

Patrolman Charles M. Hilbert
Baltimore News-American, 31 July–5 August 1950; Official Personnel Jacket, Baltimore Police Central Records Department.

Patrolman Roland W. Morgan
Baltimore News-American, 6–9 January 1951; *Baltimore Sun,* 7 January–9 January 1951; Official Personnel Jacket, Baltimore Police Central Records Department.

Sergeant James L. Scholl
Baltimore News-American, 20 July–1 August 1953; *Baltimore Sun,* 21 July–2 August 1953; Official Personnel Jacket, Baltimore Police Central Records Department.

Patrolman Alfred P. Bobelis
Baltimore News-American, 15 February 1954; *Baltimore Sun,* 15 February 1954; Official Personnel Jacket, Baltimore Police Central Records Department.

Patrolman Aubrey L. Lowman
Baltimore Sun, 19–22 April 1954; Official Personnel Jacket, Baltimore Police Central Records Department.

Patrolman Walter D. Davis
Baltimore News-American, 1–2 July 1954; *Baltimore Sun,* 3 July 1954; Official Personnel Jacket, Baltimore Police Central Records Department.

Sergeant James J. Purcell
Baltimore News-American, 24–26 October 1955; *Baltimore Sun,* 25–27 October 1955; Official Personnel Jacket, Baltimore Police Central Records Department; August Gribbin, *How It All Happened* (New York: Vantage Press, 1980).

Patrolman John R. Phelan
Baltimore News-American, 1–4 October 1956; *Baltimore Sun,* 1–4 October 1956; Official Personnel Jacket, Baltimore Police Central Records Department; August Gribbin, *How It All Happened* (New York: Vantage Press, 1980); Author interview with relative, January 2004.

Patrolman John F. Andrews
Baltimore News-American, 10–11 October 1957; Official Personnel Jacket, Baltimore Police Central Records Department.

Patrolman Robert K. Nelson
Baltimore News-American, 19–20 September 1958; Official Personnel Jacket, Baltimore Police Central Records Department.

Patrolman Richard H. Duvall, Jr.
Baltimore News-American, 12–15 January 1959; *Baltimore Sun,* 12–13 January 1959; Official Personnel Jacket, Baltimore Police Central Records Department.

Patrolman Warren V. Eckert
Baltimore News-American, 17–20 November 1960; *Baltimore Sun,* 19 November 1960; Official Personnel Jacket, Baltimore Police Central Records Department; Author interview with relative, December 2005.

Patrolman Henry Smith, Jr.
Baltimore Sun, 7–10 April 1962; Official Personnel Jacket, Baltimore Police Central Records Department.

Patrolman Richard D. Seebo
Baltimore News-American, 26 May 1962; *Baltimore Sun,* 27–30 May 1962; Official Personnel Jacket, Baltimore Police Central Records Department.

Patrolman Edward J. Kowalewski
Baltimore News-American, 2–6 July 1962; Official Personnel Jacket, Baltimore Police Central Records Department.

Patrolman Francis R. Stransky
Baltimore Sun, 12 January 1964; Official Personnel Jacket, Baltimore Police Central Records Department.

Patrolman Claude J. Profili
Baltimore Sun, 30 January–7 February 1964; Official Personnel Jacket, Baltimore Police Central Records Department.

Patrolman Walter P. Matthys
Baltimore Sun, 12–15 September 1964; Official Personnel Jacket, Baltimore Police Central Records Department.

Patrolman Teddy L. Bafford
Baltimore News-American, 16–18 October 1964; *Baltimore Sun,* 16–17 October 1964; Official Personnel Jacket, Baltimore Police Central Records Department.

Sergeant Jack L. Cooper
Baltimore Sun, 26–30 December 1964; Official Personnel Jacket, Baltimore Police Central Records Department.

Patrolman Charles R. Ernest
Baltimore Sun, 21–22 January 1965; Official Personnel Jacket, Baltimore Police Central Records Department.

Patrolman Robert H. Kuhn
Baltimore News-American, 22–24 July 1965; *Baltimore Sun,* 22–23 July 1965; Official Personnel Jacket, Baltimore Police Central Records Department.

Patrolman William J. Baumer
Baltimore Sun, 26–28 January 1967; Official Personnel Jacket, Baltimore Police Central Records Department.

Patrolman Frederick K. Kontner
Baltimore Sun, 26 January–12 February 1967; Official Personnel Jacket, Baltimore Police Central Records Department.

Patrolman John C. Williams
Baltimore Sun, 28–30 June 1967; *Baltimore Sun,* 22–23 August 1967; Official Personnel Jacket, Baltimore Police Central Records Department.

Detective Richard F. Bosak
Baltimore Sun, 19–23 April 1968; Official Personnel Jacket, Baltimore Police Central Records Department.

Patrolman George F. Heim
Baltimore Sun, 17–20 January 1970; Official Personnel Jacket, Baltimore Police Central Records Department.

Patrolman Henry M. Mickey
Baltimore Sun, 25–28 March 1970; Official Personnel Jacket, Baltimore Police Central Records Department; Baltimore Police Newsletter, Vol. 4 (8 April 1970).

Patrolman Donald W. Sager
Baltimore Sun, 25–28 April 1970; Official Personnel Jacket, Baltimore Police Central Records Department; Baltimore Police Newsletter, Vol. 4 (6 and 20 May 1970).

Patrolman Carl Peterson, Jr.
Baltimore Sun, 13 June–28 July 1971; Official Personnel Jacket, Baltimore Police Central Records Department; Baltimore Police Newsletter, Vol. 5 (16 and 30 June 1971).

Lieutenant Martin E. Webb
Baltimore Sun, 2–5 August 1971; Official Personnel Jacket, Baltimore Police Central Records Department; Baltimore Police Newsletter, Vol. 5 (11 August 1971).

Patrolman Lorenzo A. Gray
Baltimore News-American, 26–30 July 1972; *Baltimore Sun,* 26–28 July 1972; Official Personnel Jacket, Baltimore Police Central Records Department.

Patrolman Robert M. Hurley
Baltimore Sun, 29–20 March 1973; Official Personnel Jacket, Baltimore Police Central Records Department.

Patrolman Norman F. Buchman
Baltimore Sun, 7 June–7 July 1973; Official Personnel Jacket, Baltimore Police Central Records Department; Baltimore Police Newsletter, Vol. 7 (18 April and 5 September 1973).

Patrolman Calvin M. Rodwell
Baltimore Sun, 23–28 September 1973; Official Personnel Jacket, Baltimore Police Central Records Department.

Patrolman Frank W. Whitby, Jr.
Baltimore Sun, 7 April–5 May 1974; Official Personnel Jacket, Baltimore Police Central Records Department; Baltimore Police Newsletter, Vol. 8 (17 April and 15 May 1974).

Detective Sergeant Frank W. Grunder, Jr.
Baltimore Sun, 2–5 August 1974; Official Personnel Jacket, Baltimore Police Central Records Department; Baltimore Police Newsletter, Vol. 8, No. 16.

Patrolman Milton I. Spell
Baltimore Sun, 16–18 August 1974; Official Personnel Jacket, Baltimore Police Central Records Department; Baltimore Police Newsletter, Vol. 8, Nos. 17 and 18.

Patrolman Martin J. Greiner
Baltimore Sun, 1–12 December 1974; Official Personnel Jacket, Baltimore Police Central Records Department; Baltimore Police Newsletter, Vol. 8, Nos. 25 and 26.

Patrolman Edward S. Sherman
Baltimore Sun, 14–16 September 1975; Official Personnel Jacket, Baltimore Police Central Records Department; Baltimore Police Newsletter, Vol. 9, No. 20.

Patrolman Timothy B. Ridnour
Baltimore Sun, 28 October–3 November 1975; Official Personnel Jacket, Baltimore Police Central Records Department.

Patrolman Jimmy D. Halcomb
Baltimore Sun, 17–25 April 1976; Official Personnel Jacket, Baltimore Police Central Records Department; Baltimore Police Newsletter, Vol. 10, No. 9; Author interviews with relative, January 2002–June 2006.

Police Officer Edgar J. Rumpf
Baltimore Sun, 17–20 February 1978; Official Personnel Jacket, Baltimore Police Central Records Department; Baltimore Police Newsletter, Vol. 8, No. 5 and Vol 12, No. 5.

Sergeant Robert J. Barlow
Baltimore Sun, 24–25 April 1978; Official Personnel Jacket, Baltimore Police Central Records Department.

Police Officer Nelson F. Bell, Jr.
Baltimore Sun, 23–29 October 1978; Official Personnel Jacket, Baltimore Police Central Records Department; Baltimore Police Newsletter, Vol. 12, No. 23.

Police Officer William C. Albers
Baltimore Sun, 31 July–21 August 1979; Official Personnel Jacket, Baltimore Police Central Records Department; Baltimore Police Newsletter, Vol. 13, No. 18.

Police Officer Ronald Tracey
Baltimore News-American, 21–25 July 1981; *Baltimore Sun,* 21–26 July 1981; Official Personnel Jacket, Baltimore Police Central Records Department.

Detective Marcellus Ward
Baltimore Sun, 4–8 December 1984; Official Personnel Jacket, Baltimore Police Central Records Department; Baltimore Police Newsletter, Vol. 18, No. 25 and Vol. 19, No. 11; Author interview with relative, May 2006.

Police Officer Richard J. Lear
Baltimore Sun, 9–10 October 1985; Official Personnel Jacket, Baltimore Police Central Records Department; Baltimore Police Newsletter, Vol. 19. No. 21; Author interview with co-worker, September 2004.

Police Officer Vincent J. Adolfo
Baltimore Sun, 19–23 November 1985; Official Personnel Jacket, Baltimore Police Central Records Department; Baltimore Police Newsletter, Vol. 19. No. 24 and Vol. 20, No. 14; Author interview with co-worker, September 2003.

Police Officer Richard T. Miller
Baltimore Sun, 22–25 July 1986; Official Personnel Jacket, Baltimore Police Central Records Department; Baltimore Police Newsletter, Vol. 20, Nos. 13 and 16.

Police Officer Robert Alexander
Baltimore Sun, 21–25 September 1986; Official Personnel Jacket, Baltimore Police Central Records Department; Baltimore Police Newsletter, Vol. 20, No. 20; Author interview with co-worker, June 2002.

Police Officer William J. Martin
Baltimore Sun, 11–15 October 1989; Official Personnel Jacket, Baltimore Police Central Records Department; Author interview with co-worker, June 2002.

Police Officer Ira N. Weiner
Baltimore Sun, 19–23 September 1992; Official Personnel Jacket, Baltimore Police Central Records Department; Author interview with relative, January 2002–June 2006.

Police Officer Herman A. Jones, Sr.
Baltimore Sun, 27 May–2 June 1993; Official Personnel Jacket, Baltimore Police Central Records Department; Author interview with relative, January 2002–June 2006.

Police Officer Gerald M. Arminger
Baltimore Sun, 25–26 June 1994; Official Personnel Jacket, Baltimore Police Central Records Department; Author interview with co-worker, June 2002.

Lieutenant Owen E. Sweeney, Jr.
Baltimore Sun, 8–10 May 1997; Official Personnel Jacket, Baltimore Police Central Records Department; Author interview with relatives, January 2002–June 2006.

Police Officer Harold J. Carey
Baltimore Sun, 31 October–8 November 1998; Official Personnel Jacket, Baltimore Police Central Records Department.

Flight Officer Barry W. Wood
Baltimore Sun, 31 October–8 November 1998; Official Personnel Jacket, Baltimore Police Central Records Department; Author interview with relative, January 2002–June 2006.

Police Officer Jamie Roussey
Baltimore Sun, 14–18 March 2000; *Catonsville Times* 15 March 2000; Official

Personnel Jacket, Baltimore Police Central Records Department; Baltimore Police Newsletter, Vol. 34, No. 5; Author interviews with relative, January 2002–January 2005.

Police Officer Kevon M. Gavin, Sr.
Baltimore Sun, 21–28 April 2000 and 20 January 2001; Official Personnel Jacket, Baltimore Police Central Records Department.

Sergeant John D. Platt and Police Officer Kevin J. McCarthy
Baltimore Sun, 15–20 October 2000; Official Personnel Jackets. Baltimore Police Central Records Department; Author interviews with relatives, January 2002–June 2006.

Police Agent Michael A. Cowdery, Jr.
Baltimore Sun, 13–18 March 2001 and 24 May 2002; Official Personnel Jacket, Baltimore Police Central Records Department; Author interview with co-worker, January 2004.

Police Officer Crystal D. Sheffield
Baltimore Sun, 23–24 August and 18 December 2002; Official Personnel Jacket, Baltimore Police Central Records Department; Baltimore Police Newsletter, Special Edition, 4 October 2002; Author interview with relative, August 2004.

Detective Thomas G. Newman
Baltimore Sun, 22 April 2001, 24–26 November 2002, 18 February 2004, and 20 October 2004; Official Personnel Jacket, Baltimore Police Central Records Department; Baltimore Police Newsletter, Special Edition, 15 January 2003; Funeral Pamphlet; Author interview with co-worker, August 2004.

Lieutenant Walter A. Taylor
Baltimore Sun, 18 April 2003; Official Personnel Jacket, Baltimore Police Central Records Department.

Police Officer Brian D. Winder
Baltimore Sun, 4–15 July 2004; Official Personnel Jacket, Baltimore Police Central Records Department; Author interview with co-worker, November 2005.

Police Officer Anthony A. Byrd
Baltimore Sun, 19–23 May 2006; *Baltimore Examiner,* 20 May 2006; Official Personnel Jacket, Baltimore Police Central Records Department; Baltimore Police Newsletter, Special Edition, 1 June 2006; Funeral Pamphlet, Vaughn Green Funeral Home; Author interview with co-worker, June 2006.

Detective Troy Lamont Chesley
Funeral pamphlet (New Shiloh Baptist Church); *The Blue Line* Baltimore Police Newsletter, 1 February 2007 ; *Baltimore Examiner,* 9–17 January 2007; *Baltimore Sun,* 9–24 January 2007; Departmental emails retrieved on 10, 11, 13 January 2007; Interviews with co-workers; Official Departmental Personnel Jacket, Baltimore Police Central Records Department.